THE
KING'S
WARRIOR

BECOMING *the* MAN CHRIST DESIRES

THE
KING'S
WARRIOR

MATTHEW PATRICK HUGHES

Paperback: 978-1-969638-00-8
Hardcover: 978-1-969638-01-5
eBook: 978-1-969638-02-2
Audiobook: 978-1-969638-03-9

Designed by Mark Karis
Edited by Paul Higgins

CONTENTS

INTRODUCTION

INTO THE FIRE: CHRISTIANITY, MASCULINITY, AND THE WAR THAT NEVER ENDS

Before the first light scattered primordial darkness, before the world received form or foundation from the Maker's hands, a great order governed heaven's crystal heights. Within the harmony stood one adorned with splendor beyond mortal comprehension—Helel ben Shachar, the morning star, the guardian cherub who walked among stones of fire beneath the throne of the Most High (Ezekiel 28:14). Appointed to serve in sacred proximities, he knew the brilliance of divine glory and the honor of dwelling within light burning at creation's heart. Within his place of trust, something ancient turned. Desire twisted like a serpent as ambition stirred in the deeps of a once-perfect will.

With a declaration piercing heaven's order like a blade through silk, rebellion ignited across the starry hosts. "I will ascend to the heavens," he resolved with voice like thunder. "I will raise my throne above the stars of God ... I will make myself like the Most High" (Isaiah 14:13–14). The intent was treason beyond measure: to usurp heaven's ancient order, to enthrone self above the angelic company wrought to worship and serve. Pride rose like a dark tide, and with it came war the foundations had never witnessed. The dragon of old—now known as Satan—fell like lightning from heaven's heights, cast down with a third of heaven's host following his banner into shadow (Revelation 12:4, 9).

Sin's seed was sown into the cosmos like poison in a well. Cast down from crystal spheres to the young earth below, the adversary turned his fury toward his new domain. As Revelation bears witness: "The great dragon was hurled down—the ancient serpent called the devil, or Satan, leading the whole world astray. He was hurled to the earth, and his angels with him" (Revelation 12:9). The exile marked the beginning of his dominion over the circles of the world, confirmed in Job's day when Satan appeared before the throne, declaring he had been roaming the earth like a hunter stalking prey (Job 1:6–7).

Even before Job's time, in Eden's blessed garden where trees grew tall and fair, the serpent slithered through innocence, whispering deceit with honeyed tongue. Adam and Eve walked in communion with their Creator beneath paradise's golden light until the serpent challenged God's word with an alternative path: to seek knowledge independent of trust, to seize power without surrender. Eve listened to the lies, Adam followed her into shadow, and the fruit was eaten. In the moment, the sacred shattered like crystal. Fellowship was torn asunder. Through their transgression, sin entered humanity's realm, bringing death and decay. The garden was closed with flaming swords, and the very ground groaned beneath the curse.

The world of humanity became a battlefield where beauty was scarred by rebellion and glory obscured by guilt. The same war beginning in heaven's heights now rages through gardens and cities and souls. The great conflict trembles beneath every culture, shakes beneath every generation.

Even in the darkest hour, a promise rang forth from the throne of mercy. A declaration of war against the deceiver: "I will put enmity between you and the woman, and between your offspring and hers; he will crush your head, and you will strike his heel" (Genesis 3:15). The first prophecy was also the first gospel—the herald of the One who would come to reverse the curse, to restore what was lost, to reclaim what was stolen.

The One is Jesus Christ, the second Adam, the perfect Man, the eternal Word made flesh (John 1:14). Christ stands as no passive savior—He is the Warrior King, heaven's captain, the promised seed who would crush the serpent's head (Genesis 3:15).

Scripture unveils the divine champion with holy war's thundering cadence: in Exodus 15:3, "The Lord is a warrior; the Lord is His name"—a declaration forged in Egypt's deliverance and sealed by Pharaoh's chariots drowning in the Red Sea's depths. In Psalm 24:8, He is named "the Lord, strong and mighty, the Lord, mighty in battle"— the One who commands ancient gates to lift their heads as the King of Glory enters. In Isaiah 42:13, He advances like a warrior of old, stirring His zeal as a champion girded for battle—roaring like a lion awakened, prevailing with divine fury.

These are prophetic glimpses of a Savior who redeems through meekness and reigns in might, declaring triumph across the ages with both mercy and majesty. In Revelation 19:11–16, the vision stands unveiled: heaven opens like great doors of pearl, and behold—the rider on the white horse, faithful and true, crowned with many diadems, His robe dipped in blood, His name called the Word of God. From His mouth comes a sword to strike the nations, and upon His thigh is written: King of Kings and Lord of Lords.

Such glimpses reveal the majesty of the Christ who conquers with holiness and reigns through righteousness. The greatest strength stands wrapped in paradox—power cloaked in humility, judgment preceded by mercy. The same King who shall ride with fire in His eyes once walked dusty roads with earth upon His feet. The cross was chosen from divine might's fullness rather than lack thereof.

Only One truly supreme could wield infinite power and still choose sacrifice's path, walking willingly into darkness to bring forth light. For the Warrior King who bled upon the tree now reigns from heaven's throne, and the earth awaits His return—as sovereign rather than servant. No force in all the circles of the world can rival His might, and no throne can withstand His advance.

The Christ who battles darkness with glory wages war for the redeemed's sake. He took on flesh, knelt to wash feet, and bore the cross in shame—defeating death through obedience unto death rather than by legions' might.

Such humility magnifies His glory rather than diminishing its radiance. For the One who entered Jerusalem on a donkey will return crowned in fire to claim His throne upon the earth. The heel has been bruised in ancient combat, and the serpent's head shall fall beneath eternal justice. The crown of thorns shall give way to dominion's diadem. The scroll has been unsealed by the Lamb, and He who was slain now roars as the Lion of Judah.

His call now echoes across the earth like a horn blown from mountain peaks. The sword must be taken up. The war of the ages demands allegiance from every heart. The charge goes forth for the faithful as well as the strong, for courage may dwell in the smallest frame. The battlefield welcomes the willing. The fire is kindled by holy love rather than hate. And the warrior who answers carries the cause of the King.

The age groans under corruption's weight. Cities decay. Truth is traded for noise. Strength is mocked by those who know only weakness. Righteousness is ridiculed by those who walk in shadow. Still, the call goes out—to stand where others kneel, to build where others mock, to carry Christ as courage's standard rather than comfort's banner. To speak what heaven speaks, to bear what heaven bears.

The warrior of Christ is forged in the crucible. Shaped by Scripture. Strengthened by suffering. Anchored in eternity. Every life builds or breaks the Kingdom—neutrality exists only in the dreams of the willfully blind. And those who carry the King's presence must walk forward in a world resisting His reign. The task stands clear: to bear light rather than blend with shadows. To endure rather than argue with darkness. To rise each day with sword in hand and glory blazing before their eyes.

History bends toward one conclusion. The King will return, robed in righteousness, crowned with fire. Until the appointed day arrives, the war continues. And the call remains.

Rise with reverence. Build with burden. Stand with sword and Spirit. Walk as one marked by glory.

May the warrior be born.

1

THE WARRIOR'S DISCIPLINE: TRAINING THE BODY WHILE GUARDING THE HEART

Every warrior must train. The truth echoes through the halls of memory, from the first clash of sword upon shield to the quiet resolve of those who rise before dawn to test their limits. In ages past, when the world was younger and men's hearts clearer, they understood that strength was neither gift carelessly given nor treasure lightly bestowed—rather a prize hard-won through faithful labor.

Deeper still runs this ancient wisdom: that a loving father disciplines the son in whom he delights. "For the Lord disciplines the one he loves," the Scriptures declare, "and chastises every son whom he receives." The Almighty Himself, who could speak worlds into being with a word, chooses instead the patient way of trial and testing for His beloved. Love wrought through tender severity shapes gold in the fire.

So it has always been with those called to bear burdens greater than themselves. The smith's hammer rings true only after countless strikes; the archer's aim holds steady only after ten thousand arrows have found their mark. Even in the blessed realm before the Fall, dominion came through sacred toil, through the wrestling of meaning from earth and element.

The ancient fires still burn today—in gymnasiums and fields, in mountain paths and training halls—wherever mortals choose to forge themselves under their Father's watchful eye. This is where the warrior begins: with the understanding that discipline stands as a blessing crowned, a sacred burden gladly borne. For in this crucible of faithful effort, ordinary flesh reaches toward something higher, bearing at last the mark of its Maker's own unbreakable will.

Consider the shepherd boy who became king, whose story illuminates this sacred pattern. In the annals of Israel's kings, before David held a scepter, he held a sling. The pastures became his proving ground—silent hills where trumpets sounded only in heaven's register and where testing took place under the Almighty's eye. In those fields, danger arrived with formal ceremony abandoned, approaching instead with sudden teeth and claw. The lion charged David. The bear prowled at him. With undeniable faith forged long before Goliath, the boy stood firm.

These were victories wrought in flesh and bone rather than symbol and imagination. Literal flesh was torn. Adrenaline surged. The shepherd struck with precision learned through repetition rather than improvisation. His courage was cultivated through the faithful guardianship of what was entrusted to him, rather than summoned in moments of despair. As he would later testify to King Saul: "When a lion or a bear came and carried off a sheep from the flock, I went after it, struck it and rescued the sheep from its mouth" (1 Samuel 17:34–35).

Each beast driven back was a rehearsal for Goliath. Each day with the flock was preparation for the nation. The hand that protected sheep would one day wield justice over kingdoms. The harp in his grasp nurtured humility. The sling in his hand summoned valor. In this wilderness of calling, the Lord prepared His servant, as echoed in Psalm

78:70–72: "He chose David his servant and took him from the sheep pens ... to be the shepherd of his people Jacob ... and David shepherded them with integrity of heart; with skillful hands he led them."

Together, harp and sling forged a harmony between worship and warfare. The sacred and the savage met in one man. One hand sang to God, the other readied to strike for righteousness. And in that mysterious pairing—lyre and blade, praise and protection—the warrior was born.

Courts bore witness to nothing. Crowds applauded in silence. Heaven took notice. Preparation hidden from men resounded before God. Strength was summoned in solitude for stewardship rather than spectacle. In the secret places, muscles moved in obedience and spirit followed in step. The stillness was the sanctuary, the repetition the liturgy. Every private victory formed the unseen edge of a sword destined to be drawn. The cadence of the field prepared the cadence of command.

This is the pattern of heaven—strength forged in secret, tested in shadow, revealed in light. Between David's fields and the giant's fall stands the ultimate Warrior, the one who would transform training from human endeavor into divine calling. Christ entered the arena of flesh as combatant rather than spectator, taking on the same sinews and bones, the same hunger and fatigue that every man must bear.

For thirty years, the Word made flesh lived in obscurity—laboring with hands that would soon be pierced. The Carpenter who would reshape eternity first shaped wood and stone. The King who would build an eternal Kingdom first built temporal shelters. In the workshop of Nazareth, calluses formed that would one day grip the cross. Muscles strengthened that would carry the weight of the world.

The King Himself chose flesh—tendons, veins, and muscle rather than ethereal light. He walked roads. Carried burdens. Bled real blood. The Son of God, forged in carpenter's sweat, sanctified sweat for all who follow. The hands that cast galaxies shaped tables. The back that bore judgment once bore lumber. Training stood as the very path to glory—never beneath it. As Hebrews 5:8 declares, "Though He was a Son, He learned obedience by the things which He suffered."

Every field of preparation echoes in eternity. The body was designed as a vessel for divine glory. "Do you know that your bodies are temples of the Holy Spirit?" Paul declares (1 Corinthians 6:19). Sanctuaries for heaven's habitation—sacred dwellings wherein the Almighty makes His abode. The flesh disciplined becomes a faithful ally. The flesh indulged becomes a traitor within the gates.

True training runs deeper than muscle and bone. It reaches into the hidden places where character is hammered into form. The warrior who knows hunger learns to distinguish want from need. The frame that knows fatigue discovers reserves that weakness never suspects. The hands that know calluses can grasp what soft palms cannot hold.

This is training as Trinity intended—body, mind, and spirit aligned under Christ's command. The body disciplined through sacred effort. The mind renewed through the Word of God. The spirit surrendered through prayer and worship. When all three move in harmony, they become a mirror of heaven's design—mortality reflecting divine unity.

The flesh properly trained serves righteousness. The mind properly renewed speaks truth. The spirit properly surrendered carries presence. Together, they form neither mere warrior nor common vessel—rather an instrument of glory, prepared for works prepared beforehand.

Physical training alone produces only physical results. The warrior who builds only muscle while neglecting the inner man has constructed a temple with neither god to inhabit it nor weapon with cause to wield it nor vessel with purpose to fulfill.

The hour approaches when the King will call. The enemy already prowls. The field awaits the warrior who has learned to train for the approval of heaven rather than the applause of men. Let the training begin where all true strength begins—on the knees before the throne of the One who calls ordinary men to extraordinary purpose.

The warrior's discipline concerns the King he serves above all earthly consideration. And that King—who trained in obscurity, who fasted in the wilderness, who carried the cross to Calvary—desires His faithful to follow in His example.

2

THE FALSE ALTAR OF
PAIN AND BLOOD

Warriors sometimes mistake the forge for punishment. Beneath iron and repetition, beneath silence between breaths, a shadowed altar rises—unseen by some men, and false to all. Discipline driven by guilt, carved from desperate hope that enough human sweat might wash away what only Christ's blood can cleanse.

The body, once a temple, becomes a tribunal. Repetitions transform into penances paid to false gods masquerading as self-help ideologies. "Perhaps this rep will silence the past. Perhaps this weight will crush the memory. Perhaps enough blood in my mouthpiece will drown the ache within."

This is a ridiculous mentality.

Behold a key component to the dangerous modern belief system, this false religion of grind upon the altar of anguish. A false priesthood where pain holds the blade and guilt conducts the choir. The self-bastardizing world (ever eager for meaning without submission to its Father) applauds such sacrifice—mistaking torment for tenacity, performance for purpose. Even the Church may nod, confusing relentless discipline with spiritual devotion.

False altars rise whenever the soul seeks healing apart from surrender to Christ. They are adorned with the language of self-help and self-mastery, echoing the age-old lie that man can fix what is fractured without heaven's intervention. While the mirror reflects effort, the soul grows weary beneath its glare. The bar keeps rising. Peace never lands. Disciplines meant to heal become liturgies of condemnation. All the while, the altar appears clean—the offering remains unacceptable.

The first false altar was built east of Eden, where Cain laid his offering before the Lord. It represented toil—the hard-earned fruit of his labor and the sweat of hard effort. This toil-soaked sweat tainted his offering. Abel, however, brought the firstborn of his flock in sincere faith, and only in sincere faith. His offering was not born of toil, while Cain offered the work of his hands out of pride. One offering showed dependence; the other expressed independence, as Abel relied on the means the Lord provided, while Cain believed his effort was what God wanted.

Heaven's response split the earth: "The Lord looked with favor on Abel and his offering, but on Cain and his offering he did not look with favor" (Genesis 4:4–5). The altar built on effort stood exposed next to the altar built on trust, and in that moment, the inadequacy of self-reliance shone brightly like lightning in a clear sky.

Cain's heart burned—from exposure rather than injustice. His offering, shaped by toil and pride, had been rejected—for its lack of surrender rather than its appearance. Abel's offering reflected trust in what God required, a blood sacrifice foreshadowing grace.

Cain lacked the posture of dependence. His hands worked, but his heart stayed closed. When heaven's favor came through faith rather than effort, Cain's disillusionment turned into fury. Instead of repenting, Cain raged and struck his brother dead. Abel's blood soaked the ground—because Abel's obedience showed the truth: faith in God overrides any labor, an idea for which he was martyred. It is faith—rather than labor—which will open heaven's gates upon one's arrival to them.

This is where false altars create an illusion. They demand sacrifice without offering peace. They exhaust the body and starve the soul. These altars lure through self-improvement, declaring effort holy while passively turning the heart away from God. These false altars may whisper promises of freedom through discipline, of healing through grind, while constantly shifting the focus from the cross to the self. What starts as a desire to grow can be hijacked into a plan to replace faith with works, and in that exchange, the soul drifts away from the only One who can truly restore it.

When heaven's favor fell on faith, Cain's face fell in fury. Jealousy boiled. Rage rose. The grind had failed to gain glory. So when faith stood beside effort, Cain raised his hand. Abel fell beneath the wrath of works.

This is how false altars develop. What starts as a gift turns into a parasite. These altars contain the seeds of destruction—for others and for the soul that creates them. They transform men into slaves of effort and enemies of grace. Like Cain's altar, every modern altar built apart from surrender faces the same outcome: distance from God, distortion of identity, and a heart still wandering east of Eden.

The Scriptures declare a better way. "By grace you have been saved through faith ... not by works, so that no one may boast" (Ephesians 2:8–9). The blood has already been shed. The sacrifice has already been made. The Lamb has already been slain (Revelation 5:6).

Pain, when entrusted to the Redeemer, becomes refinement. As with gold in the furnace, the soul grows radiant through righteous trial (1 Peter 1:6–7). Suffering bears fruit when sown in faith—producing perseverance, then character, then hope (Romans 5:3–4). Even the heaviest cross, lifted in trust, becomes preparation for glory. Grace alone redeems.

The altar of Christ bears no demand for repayment—only invitation. Blood was already spilled. Freedom already purchased. The warrior who approaches such an altar comes to receive worth from above, rather than attempting to prove himself.

But here stands the choice that defines every man: Which altar will you approach? Which kingdom will you serve?

The false altar whispers of self-made glory, promising that enough effort can earn what grace freely gives. The true altar declares a different truth—that the work is finished, the victory won, the King already crowned. One demands you prove your worth through blood and sweat. The other proclaims your worth was proven through nail-scarred hands.

The warrior who abandons the false altar must still choose where to pledge his allegiance. For every man serves some kingdom—whether built by his own hands or established by the King of kings. Training becomes sacred ground only when the surrender precedes the sweat, when discipline flows from devotion rather than desperation.

3

FIGHTING FOR THE RIGHT KINGDOM

Every battle begins in the heart. Before fists clench or swords rise, something awakens beneath the surface—ambition, loyalty, desire. "Above all else, guard your heart, for everything flows from it" (Proverbs 4:23). When that desire becomes misaligned, even the most noble crusade becomes a march toward ruin. The warrior must ask: Whose kingdom is being built?

Every fight is holy. Every campaign is consecrated. Sacrifice can be a masquerade, veiling pride in the armor of purpose. Discernment must come before warfare. The heart must be searched, the motive tested, and the call clarified in the presence of the King. The warrior follows the Commander rather than choosing the battle. The victory belongs to the Lord (Proverbs 21:31), and blades should be drawn with His banner raised.

The path forward demands calibration of will and soul. Righteousness is forged through proximity to the Righteous One. Drawing near to Christ, the warrior receives clarity. The soul rests in divine commission rather than lurching toward self-made missions. The voice of the Spirit resounds clearer than the cries of ambition. As written, "He has shown you, O man, what is good ... to do justice, love mercy, and walk humbly with your God" (Micah 6:8).

This alignment marks the beginning of true calling. Purpose springs from stillness before the throne rather than striving amongst mortals. The warrior is sent rather than driven. Strength carried into battle flows from the presence of the King Himself rather than adrenaline or applause.

The kingdom of self rises subtly—draped in respectable discipline and adorned with applause. A noble goal, once pure, begins to crave recognition. Ambition replaces adoration. What once moved at the whisper of heaven now swells with pride. The warrior forgets the altar where surrender was sealed and starts to draw strength from performance, visibility, and applause.

Aligning with Christ means forfeiting the banner of ego, tearing down the emblems of self-promotion, and lifting high the standard of the King. Under Christ's banner, purpose regains purity, and the sword finds its rightful place—wielded for righteousness rather than self-justification. In surrender, the warrior's cause becomes sanctified. Motives align with heaven. The armor is fastened in preparation for divine commission rather than pursuit of personal conquest.

The Kingdom of God emerges from consecrated hands and reverent hearts. Thrones of men crumble, while Christ reigns from within the soul that yields. "Seek first the kingdom of God and His righteousness," Christ declared (Matthew 6:33). Obedience alone sustains what altars of acclaim cannot uphold. Every stone laid for the Kingdom must be set in surrender. Every battle waged must echo with the King's will— purposed through communion rather than merely permitted. When the heart aligns with Christ, the warrior steps into battles chosen by heaven, perfectly placed in the cadence of grace.

David was anointed long before being enthroned. Chosen by God for the throne because his heart aligned with the heart of heaven (1 Samuel 13:14), David carried the oil of kingship into caves, served enemies with integrity, and withheld his hand when shortcuts to power demanded disobedience. David's victories bore the mark of obedience rather than applause. Measured by the One who sees in secret rather than by men. Even when the throne seemed within reach, David chose the wilderness rather than violate the command of the Lord (1 Samuel 24:6). This is the pattern of the right kingdom—authority flowing from alignment, and greatness bowing before God's timing.

The warrior must search the battlefield within. Is the labor truly worship, or is it a negotiation for worth? Is the prayer a cry for His will, or a veil for personal gain? The Kingdom of heaven is built on motives rooted in Christ rather than self. Names cannot be carved into the foundation alongside His. Glory belongs to One.

The test comes daily. In silence. In secret. The challenge of dethroning the self. This throne must be surrendered morning by morning, decision by decision. In yielding the weight of personal plans and laying aside every crown of self, alignment is forged—through surrender rather than striving. From that sacred place, true purpose rises. The assignment once imagined becomes redefined under divine light. What was once built in isolation finds its place in the greater architecture of the Kingdom.

The warrior of Christ marches forward in alignment rather than for renown. A vision of the King has quieted the need for applause. A taste of holy fire has dimmed every lesser hunger. From this awakening, ambition surrenders its crown, and the altar is swept clean of self.

In this place of yielding, alignment is born. The soul steadies under the banner of righteousness rather than being pulled by performance. Eyes fix upon the Commander. The King's banner rises high above the heart's worn battlements, drawing forth divine courage from consecration.

From such alignment, unbreakable strength is born. This is the ground of legacy—the foundation of purpose which endures beyond breath. Let the warrior stand, wholly given, utterly aligned, stepping forward into the battles chosen by heaven. The aligned are truly assigned, and the assigned shall stand tall in righteous victory when the dust of spiritual warfare clears and the King of Glory comes for His eternal throne.

4

THE FALSE COMPASS:
DIRECTION WITHOUT CHRIST

The greatest danger is not always in rebellion. Sometimes it hides in resolve—a steady march guided by oneself rather than surrender. Often, men fail to recognize when they've missed their target. They stray because of wounds, ego, fear, or ambition cloaked in reverence. The compass slowly drifts, influenced by performance, pain, pride, or applause.

While hands stay busy and voices speak Scripture, hearts veer silently off course. Confidence aimed in the wrong direction proves more treacherous than recklessness. Their compass remains intact, merely miscalibrated. Without Christ, direction vanishes. Without direction, journey becomes impossible—only motion in circles remains.

The heart of man longs for purpose. When God's presence is absent, this longing turns inward. The modern warrior trains in hustle, self-optimization, and relentless self-determination. He reads books, crushes routines, posts progress. But without surrender, even excellence becomes idolatry. He climbs—yet toward what end? He sets goals—for whose glory? He improves—though who is glorified in the transformation? Many are improving while remaining unchanged. Many are disciplined while staying lost.

They believe they are growing, though the fruit proves hollow. The leaves appear green while the root remains absent. The danger exceeds a man who sins—it encompasses a man who succeeds without God and assumes success is God. He moves faster, gets stronger, earns more—while remaining equally distant from heaven. Direction flows from presence, never from momentum.

Scripture overflows with men who started well and wandered. The erosion came through gradual autonomy rather than open rebellion. They replaced guidance with instinct. The compass drifted. The fire dimmed. Yet they pressed on, too proud to stop, too confident to recalibrate. To lose your way is tragedy—to convince yourself you haven't is delusion.

To follow Christ transcends simply being clean—it means being led. Many lay down lust, anger, addiction—while keeping control. They offer Christ their habits while withholding their horizons. They are repentant in behavior while remaining autonomous in spirit. Christ shares no throne with mortal pride.

True disciples are yielded rather than merely righteous. Their movements flow from communion rather than clarity. They march only when the Presence goes before them, never simply because the path appears open. Like Israel in the wilderness, they follow the cloud by day and fire by night—not because the land is easy, but because the Presence is near (Exodus 13:21–22).

This Presence often leads where pride refuses to go. Into valleys. Into silence. Into unknown lands ruled by giants and guarded by walls. When the twelve spies surveyed Canaan, ten reported through fear. Only Joshua and Caleb spoke through faith (Numbers 13:27–33). The land was rich, yes. The cities were fortified. The people were giants. Yet Joshua and Caleb remained steadfast in the Father's promise. They acknowledged the challenge while magnifying the God who had split seas and rained bread from heaven. For them, the cloud had not moved. If the Presence remained, then the promise stood firm.

This marks the difference between those who are driven and those who are led. Driven men force doors open. Led men wait for the cloud to lift. Driven men make things happen. Led men move when God speaks. Driven men pursue comfort or conquest. Led men pursue communion. The former may gain the world. The latter inherit a Kingdom.

Saul's downfall began in impatience rather than rebellion. He feared God's silence more than man's disapproval. So he moved ahead of the prophet and lost the Kingdom. David fell not because he lacked worship, but because he hid. His strength failed when he stopped confessing. Peter denied Christ from fear rather than hatred—when he trusted instinct more than identity.

Each man stepped into shadow the moment he stopped being led.

Yet none were discarded forever. God disciplines, but He does not discard. He wounds, but He heals. He corrects, but He restores. Even when the compass fails, the Shepherd does not. He finds the warrior— broken, breathless, ashamed—and offers the same invitation He gave to Peter, to David, to every man who has strayed: "Follow Me."

The true compass of the warrior is neither a clever life plan nor productive habits. It is an altar. A place where dreams are not buried to rot but surrendered to rise. Where selfish ambition dies so holy desire may live. Where plans are not discarded but refined. Where direction is not decided but discerned. "Direct my footsteps according to Your word," David prayed, "let no sin rule over me" (Psalm 119:133).

This compass is forged in quiet chambers of surrender—in still places where ego dies and God alone defines direction. A warrior trained in surrender does not ask, "Is this working?" or "Is this wise?" He asks, "Is this from the Lord?" And if the answer is silence, he waits.

The places appearing barren may be holy. The detours may be protection. The delays may be mercy in disguise. God is not bound by efficiency. He is bound by love. The warrior who is led will find though the path may wind, the Shepherd never wanders.

Christ never promised ease. He promised alignment. He never guaranteed that following would lead to fame or comfort or clarity. He promised it would lead to Him. And where He leads, there will always be a cross.

Yet at the foot of this cross, the warrior finds what no man can forge for himself: peace surpassing understanding, strength made perfect in weakness, and dreams not diminished—but fulfilled beyond imagining.

5

THE BATTLE OF THE MIND, BODY, AND SPIRIT

A warrior may charge forward with steel gleaming and valor blazing in his eyes, yet remain sundered within his own fortress. He fortifies flesh while neglecting thought, trains sinew while abandoning soul, bows his head in prayer while secretly permitting strongholds to flourish in shadowed silence. Though appearing whole to every watching eye, inwardly he stands fractured—fighting as scattered host rather than unified man, unaware that the most perilous enemies whisper from chambers within his own heart.

The Word of the Almighty permits no such division. Scripture speaks to man in his entirety, summoning him beyond mere resistance against evil toward complete alignment with his Creator's design. Holiness dwells in wholeness alone. Holiness refuses fragmentation. The man bearing God's image must live in unity, for the God who formed him exists as three-in-one.

As Father, Son, and Spirit dwell in perfect communion, so the warrior carries a trinitarian imprint—mind, body, and spirit. Each part distinct. Each part sacred. Each fashioned for cooperation rather than competition in divine purpose. When all three move in harmony, offered together before the Throne, they become heaven's mirror—a mortal reflection of eternal unity.

The battle begins within the mind—the battleground of thought and identity where internal war commences long before any sword is drawn. The enemy arrives bearing subtle distortions: questions masquerading as reason, memories twisted through shame's alchemy, truths laced with poison's kiss. He whispers, "Did God really say?" (Genesis 3:1), and beneath the warrior's feet, solid ground begins its treacherous shift. Thought becomes agreement, agreement transforms into identity, identity births behavior, and behavior forges bondage's chains.

Paul commands us to "take every thought captive to make it obedient to Christ" (2 Corinthians 10:5). Every thought—never merely some. Should the warrior fail to command this citadel which is the mind, the enemy shall claim dominion. Every belief rooted in fear's soil, every assumption born from trauma's womb, every self-imposed label forged in rejection's furnace must fall like strongholds torn down by siege engines. The warrior who loses the war of the mind shall lose every subsequent battle.

Appetite must never rule the body; fatigue may never justify surrender. Flesh demands training for valor rather than vanity, consecration rather than competition. The physical realm intertwines with spiritual warfare rather than separate from it. The warrior who yields flesh to laziness or lust finds his spirit dulled, his edge lost to time's erosion.

Beyond flesh, beyond thought, dwells the spirit—man's inner sanctuary where God's breath animates the frame. Here communion begins, discernment awakens, identity receives its seal, and peace finds its anchor. Many men carry knowledge while maintaining empty spirits. They speak prayers without meeting their God. They attend worship while avoiding intimacy's demands. Yet the spirit yields to neither fabrication nor manipulation through noise or spectacle. Surrender alone awakens the spirit; abiding alone strengthens its resolve.

When the spirit quickens to life, all else follows its lead. The deceiving fog in the mind clears. The man abides rather than performing, yields rather than striving. He becomes integrated beyond mere efficiency, sanctified beyond simple productivity.

This restoration stands as Christ's death-purchased gift. He died to raise whole men rather than fractured souls limping between strength and shame. The renewed man brings thoughts, limbs, and soul under the Lordship of his Creator. He becomes the Trinity's vessel and reflection.

When this trinitarian reflection of man rises, darkness trembles before approaching danger.

A man with a renewed mind cannot suffer deception's arrows.

Yet let the warrior receive this warning: fragmentation's temptations shall return. Thoughts will wander through forbidden paths. Flesh will crave forbidden pleasures. In such moments, the man faces temptation to offer effort rather than presence, performance rather than intimacy, discipline divorced from devotion. These self-made altars crack under pressure; and only grace's altar bears the full weight of humanity.

So let the warrior rise again as Christ arose—renewed and whole. Let him return bearing surrender as his banner. The war he fights rages against every force seeking to divide what God has come to restore.

When a man's thoughts receive renewal, his body finds submission, and his spirit awakens to its calling, he achieves more than Trinity's reflection—he aligns himself with Trinity's eternal dance.

6

LEADING WITH STRENGTH, HUMILITY, AND DISCIPLINE

Upon the warrior's back rests the weight of souls entrusted to his care. In God's Kingdom, leadership stands as a righteous burden carried rather than a ladder climbed. Heaven entrusts such weight to the obedient and the surrendered. The true mark of leadership is how many people rise in Christ because of that leader's efforts, rather than how many bow before their throne.

Leadership comes from the dirt and salt of the earth rather than descending from thrones.

Christ taught leadership through lowliness rather than tactics or titles. On the night betrayal shadowed his steps, when fear scattered his friends like autumn leaves, the Son of God took basin and towel to wash the feet of his disciples—including feet that would soon carry betrayal to his door (John 13:3–5). The One most filled with glory served most willingly. Through that kneeling posture, Christ forever redefined the essence of leadership.

To lead in the Kingdom means carrying burdens beyond one's own. Leadership flows as stewardship rather than self-preservation. The leader bears a Name rather than builds one. "Stewards must be found faithful" (1 Corinthians 4:2). The leader's voice prioritizes the Word over personal direction. Legacy is secondary to being faithfully obedient.

The shepherd leads through faithfulness rather than flawlessness. The shepherd stays when others flee. Remains when misunderstood. Carries when others collapse. Disciplines from love rather than pride. Speaks truth for restoration rather than victory. When people stray, the shepherd calls them home rather than shames their wandering.

The warrior-leader nurtures disciples rather than chases crowds. The leader walks slowly enough to be followed, boldly enough to inspire trust. Life becomes a living map pointing toward Christ rather than oneself. "Follow me, as I follow Christ" (1 Corinthians 11:1), Paul wrote. Therein lies the tension in Kingdom leadership: vulnerability paired with steadiness, honesty combined with holiness, wounds that earn trust.

Christ remains the model. The Shepherd who leaves ninety-nine for the one (Luke 15:4). The Master who restores fallen disciples with breakfast and mercy (John 21:15–17). The King whose crown bore thorns rather than gold. Whose throne rose on cross rather than carved from ivory. Christ ruled through dying rather than dominance. Led through descent rather than demand—lower, deeper, until becoming servant of all.

The weight of leadership bears heavily. Yet the carrier bears this weight alongside Another. Christ goes before. The Spirit strengthens. Heaven watches and whispers approval. Praise becomes unnecessary when one voice matters—the voice alone that counts:

"Well done, good and faithful servant" (Matthew 25:21).

7

THE ARMOR OF GOD: PREPARING
FOR SPIRITUAL BATTLE

Warriors move forward cautiously. Though unseen by mortal eyes, the battlefield stretches far—woven into daily routines, threaded through ordinary hours. The adversary comes like wind through wheat—subtle, searching, yet relentless. The enemy slips between thoughts, stands at the edge of memory, listens for fatigue, and watches for hesitation.

A potential defeat often stems from a lack of preparation. A heart full of zeal may charge ahead, vulnerable, and become a target. Fire kindled by devotion fades when left to face the storm alone.

The voice of the apostle, ancient and eternal, breaks through the noise: "Put on the whole armor of God" (Ephesians 6:11). This stands as heaven's rallying cry, a call to wear divine craftsmanship. Each piece forged by grace. Every strap fitted with wisdom. Every seam woven with strength.

Armor stands as the necessity of the prepared. Crisis awaits usefulness; armor is worn in stillness so the soul may endure the shaking. This stands as covenant attire. Heaven's response to the war that wages quietly beneath the surface of all things.

The enemy studies movements and patterns—the slow erosion of conviction, the unchecked glance, the prayer delayed. The adversary reads the rhythm of a man's day, and where armor is absent, the enemy attempts to plant subtle seeds that bloom in silence.

Each piece was fashioned in fire and sealed by the breath of the King. Every layer carries memory, covenant, and promise. All fastenings draw soul and spirit into alignment with the eternal.

The belt encircles everything, binding the truth around the core so that any part that may stray is kept in place. The breastplate rests over the heart—protecting what is cherished, what is believed, and what is becoming. The shoes are shod with peace—presence—making every step steady through scorched or sacred ground. The shield rises like a wall in the wind, turning aside fiery whispers that aim to lodge lies in the soul. The helmet crowns the mind with clarity, divinely aligning vision and thought in salvation's promise. The sword exists as the breath of God, piercing darkness with every word spoken in faith.

This is the regalia of sons who bear the weight of glory. This stands as the armor of those who walk for allegiance. Those who remember the name carved upon their spirit by the hand of heaven.

To wear this armor is to live in the light. To carry fire in a realm grown cold.

THE BELT OF TRUTH

"I am the way, and the truth, and the life. No one comes to the Father except through me" (John 14:6).

The battle begins at the center. The warrior may bear a breastplate, lift a shield, or swing a sword—yet when the belt is loose, everything collapses.

This belt stands as the first fastening, the hidden strength that gathers all into order. The belt encircles the core with clarity. The belt draws armor into place. The belt anchors the soul in alignment. When this is secure, everything else holds firm.

Truth, genuine truth, remains timeless. Immovable. Wild as fire and pure as spring water flowing down from the heights. Truth stands as the language of heaven, the breath of the Word, the foundation upon which the universe stands.

In this present age, truth is traded like a coin—refined to suit preference, repackaged to comfort the crowd. Voices rise from every direction, each calling their echo reality.

However, truth is objective reality. It has always been and will always be, just as the Father has always been and always will be. For the Father and the Son and the Spirit are the truth.

So the belt is fastened. Pulled tight around the soul. In a world swirling with partial truths and hollow slogans, this binding cord calls the man back to the center. Back to holiness. Back to the King. When temptation rises with honeyed lies, the belt holds fast. When silence tempts compromise, the belt stabilizes courage from the truth. When chaos fills the day like smoke, this truth clears the air.

Fasten the belt daily. Wrap the belt around the soul with reverence. For when the warrior walks girded in truth, the warrior walks in step with He who shaped the stars.

THE BREASTPLATE OF RIGHTEOUSNESS

"For out of the heart come evil thoughts—murder, adultery, sexual immorality, theft, false testimony, slander. These are what defile a person ..." (Matthew 15:19–20).

The heart stands as a furnace and a fountain. From the heart rise the songs of worship and the whispers of temptation. In its depths dwell convictions that guide, wounds that speak, and desires that shape the course of a man's life. Yet evil can flow from this hidden place when it is left untended. Therefore, the warrior must guard the heart with the breastplate of righteousness.

The breastplate stands as the armor laid across the heart—the chamber of longing, memory, and devotion. It rests over the center of the warrior's being, forged in the heat of battle upon the altar of mercy. Shaped by divine hands, this piece stands as a vestment of grace—fitted for the pardoned.

Righteousness is the robe of the redeemed—freely given, graciously bestowed. Righteousness stands as the inheritance of the lowly who kneel before the Lamb and rise washed in something they could never have woven for themselves. It covers the soul like snow over ash to declare: this one has been made clean.

In this righteous breastplate, the heart finds refuge. When old guilt claws at memory and shame prowls like a lion in the long hours of night, the breastplate holds firm. The weight reminds the soul that it is anchored in something far deeper than self-effort. The enemy may speak the truth of a man's past, yet righteousness speaks the greater truth of Christ's finished work.

Beneath the covering beats a heart reborn. A heart that once longed for praise now longs for purity. A heart that once wandered through many voices now listens for one. A heart that once bowed to lesser kings now stands upright, ruled by truth and love. The affections are refined. The compass recalibrated.

To wear the breastplate is to live in consecration. To speak from a place of peace. To choose what is noble when the easy path beckons. To stand from pride from position, anchored in what has been spoken from above. The warrior is steady because the warrior is unscathed because the warrior has been secured.

Fasten the breastplate across the heart. Let the breastplate guard your waking thoughts and your midnight prayers. Let the breastplate soak in worship, let the breastplate be polished with repentance. Let the breastplate remind you daily that you are your own—you were bought with blood, and your heart now bears the seal of the Everlasting One.

THE SHOES OF THE GOSPEL OF PEACE

"Peace I leave with you; my peace I give to you. I do not give to you as the world gives. Let your hearts be steady and unafraid" (John 14:27).

These shoes of the Gospel of peace serve as a foundation—crafted by the hands of the King, soaked in the message of the Gospel, woven with the stillness of heaven's peace. With every step, the shoes carry presence into places long claimed by shadows.

This peace is profound—grounded in the authority of Christ, who faced the storm and spoke, and the waves calmly obeyed Him. The same voice that calmed the sea now soothes the soul. And the warrior who walks in this peace becomes a vessel of that same calming fire.

These shoes carry a message born in blood and raised in glory. The peace of the Gospel is neither confined to pulpits or parchment but indeed walks. It moves across valleys, into homes, through prisons, onto battlefields. Wherever the feet of the faithful touch, the claim of Christ is already declared: This, too, belongs to the Kingdom.

Each stride is deliberate, each step a prayer. With these shoes, the Gospel travels the world.

The road beneath may be scorched, the terrain uncertain, the mission heavy. Still, the steps remain firm. These shoes remember the One who washed His disciples' feet, who walked through crowds with compassion, who carried the cross up the hill.

Bind these shoes with reverence each morning. Let the dust of the day find the shoes faithful. Let the paths you walk, whether wide or winding, be marked by peace that wavers and truth that fades. For the warrior whose feet carry the Good News carries more than a message.

The warrior carries the march of a Kingdom advancing.

THE SHIELD OF FAITH

"In all circumstances take up the shield of faith, with which you can extinguish all the flaming darts of the evil one" (Ephesians 6:16).

There are arrows in this life—flaming, precise, and relentless spiritual weaponry. The arrows come through words unspoken and voices that linger long after they should have faded. They ride the wind of memory and fall in silence upon the soul. Doubt. Shame. Delay. The haunting ache that creeps in just before dawn. These are accidents. These are drawn, aimed, and loosed with cunning.

And so, the warrior lifts the shield.

The shield is forged in the fires of God's faithfulness—layered in every promise kept, every deliverance remembered, every silent night endured with breath still in the lungs. The shield stands as the quiet might of trust which has been tested and tried.

Faith is the rock upon which hope is established. Faith stands as the spine of the soul, the steady gaze in the storm. Faith bases itself like an ancient tree—rooted deep, unmoved by the howl of wind. Faith races ahead. Faith stands. And when the enemy's flame comes to consume, faith rises like a wall, and the fire dies upon the surface.

This shield carries stories.

Each scar upon the frame is a remembrance of moments when the Spirit victoriously deflected evil.

And when arms grow heavy, when the shield begins to slip—grace meets there.

Lift the shield at the whisper of fear and in the silence of temptation. Let the shield rise when the battlefield stretches wide and the day feels long. Let the shield rise when memory accuses and vision fades. Let the shield rise even when hands tremble—for in that trembling God's strength shines through.

THE HELMET OF SALVATION

"But let us who live in the light be clearheaded, protected by the armor
of faith and love, and wearing as our helmet the confidence of our
salvation" (1 Thessalonians 5:8).

The mind is a battlefield of its own. Long before the sword is drawn,
long before feet move, long before hands reach for shield or flame, the
battle begins in thought.

And so, the warrior puts on the helmet.

The helmet rests with purpose, adorned with divine decoration.
Placed gently upon the head by the hand of the Father, the helmet is
shaped to secure the place where stories are remembered and fears are
conquered. The helmet is formed in assurance—the steady knowing
that redemption has already come, that grace has already been poured
out, and that the battle, though fierce, decides the final song.

The helmet wraps around the mind like morning light, casting out
the chill of lies whispered in the long watches of night. The helmet
silences illegitimate thought and teaches the mind to rest in the divine
intellect of the Father who forged the piece.

For the world speaks loudly. And the enemy speaks often. Their
voices come cloaked in half-truths, with words that mimic wisdom yet
bear the fruits of fear. The voices speak of delay and disqualification.
They attempt to remind the soul of what was done, and what was
broken, and what still feels too far gone.

Praise the Lord and fear not! Salvation speaks louder, though salvation rarely raises its voice. Salvation simply remains as it is universally
bestowed upon all via the crucifixion.

The helmet guards the vision and shields the perspective. When
despair clouds the horizon, salvation lifts the gaze. When confusion
thickens like smoke, salvation clears the air. When the enemy whispers,
"You are still that man," the helmet responds, "You have been made new."

To wear the helmet is to know of oneself as already redeemed.

Fasten the helmet gently and firmly. Wear the helmet in prayer. Let the dawning of the helmet bring Christ's over your thoughts as dawn rests over dark hills. Let the helmet soften your fears and sharpen your sight. For the warrior who walks with salvation over the mind walks with eternity seated just above the brow—and any voice can unwrite what grace has already spoken.

THE SWORD OF THE SPIRIT

> "For the word of God is living and active, sharper than any two-edged sword... piercing to the division of soul and spirit, of joints and marrow, and discerning the thoughts and intentions of the heart" (Hebrews 4:12).

There comes a time when standing by is no longer acceptable. In those moments, the warrior must draw the sword.

The sword stands as the breath of God, spoken and living. The Sword of the Spirit is the Word as Presence.

This sword's edge is sharpened by prayer through reverent repetition during the quiet watches of morning. By hiding truth in the heart, where truth remains—dormant and waiting. Ready to emerge.

Christ Himself wielded the sword in the wilderness. When the adversary twisted Scripture into shadow, the Son responded, "It is written." With those words, the sword was drawn. In anger. In clarity. And the serpent recoiled.

The warrior does the same. When the time comes—when lies encircle, when weariness whispers, when the soul starts to tremble—the warrior unsheathes the Word. And darkness remembers fear.

When spoken in faith, the Word does what the force of no man can do—the Word reaches both soul and marrow. The Word cuts away the false self to awaken the true one.

To carry this weapon is to carry the voice of God Himself.

THE CALL TO BE FULLY ARMORED

The armor stands as a gift forged for endurance, purpose, and holy align-ment. Each piece bears the breath of its Maker, designed for comfort in His covenant. When worn with intention, the armor protects and transforms the vessel it occupies.

To be fully armored is to be fully awakened to the weight of divine calling.

The belt is drawn first—truth wrapped around the soul like a song of order. The belt fastens identity into alignment, securing every piece with strength that never fades. In the presence of truth, any confusion loses its voice. The foundation is held firm beneath the warrior's frame.

Across the chest lies the breastplate of righteousness. The breastplate protects the sacred inner self, where conviction is ignited in the heart and love is nurtured. This covering shields said heart, allowing it to beat freely in harmony with grace, steady in both calm seas and stormy.

Peace rests upon the feet. These are the shoes that carry the Gospel with quiet fire—walking through cities and silence, deserts and sanc-tuaries. Wherever the shoes tread, so does hope. The message they carry is one of beauty and boldness: reconciliation has arrived, and heaven is near.

The shield rises like a wall against despair. Forged from faith, layered with trust, and held in quiet defiance of fear, this shield bears the marks of every trial weathered and every promise kept. The shield is lifted with force, with remembrance. Every movement with the shield declares the presence of one who believes.

Upon the brow, the helmet of salvation is crowned. This stands as a symbol of arrival, the steady flame of belonging. Salvation brings clarity to the mind and calls the soul into deeper assurance.

In the hand and carried with reverence is the sword of the Spirit: the Word of God. Alive, breathing, and unyielding. A blade that cuts through shadows with a whisper of truth. The edge alone brings healing and destruction. Its strength lies in its volume of faith. When spoken in stillness, the sword reshapes worlds.

This stands as the inheritance of the entrusted. Each piece reflects the nature of the King: righteous, ready, and radiant.

The individual fully armored bears more than just defense; they carry a sacred mission.

For the warrior, the Word turns into action, the Spirit transforms into power, and God's plan appears among people. Though the battle has ended, the armor remains, and the King continues to move forward through those who wear it well.

8

THE CALL TO BUILD: LEGACY IN A WORLD THAT TEARS DOWN

A sacred moment arrives when the clash of steel fades and the sword finds its rest. Healing begins. Strength returns. The King speaks again—not a whisper this time, but a holy summons deep as thunder:

Build.

A great transformation begins. Endurance yields to vision. What once simply existed to resist now bows to shape. The ground beneath the victor's feet, once trampled by war, reveals itself as fertile soil. From that soil, something eternal rises. Legacy takes root in remembrance and quiet inheritance.

The Kingdom breathes through the hearts of builders. In stillness, they hear heaven's rhythm and respond with steady hands. To build is to wage physical peace with stone and breath. Where the world forgets the future, they prepare it. Each lifted beam echoes hope. Each restored altar declares God's nearness. Though unseen by many, such labor sings in the courts of heaven.

The one who builds carries a spirit of renewal. In broken places, beauty returns. Vision replaces ruins. Hands once used to shield now hold steady as walls rise. Voices may mock. Resistance may come. Yet each step forward breathes defiance against despair.

The builder does not turn from ruin. He enters it with clear eyes and ready spirit. He collects scattered stones, gathers forgotten dreams, and breathes prayer into foundations. The altar rises once more, each layer a hymn of belonging.

The work is slow yet sacred. Often hidden. Often heavy. Hands ache. Voices fade. Still, the labor continues. Legacy grows from the daily choice to return, to remain, to endure with reverent resolve.

It forms in moments of patience, in acts of mercy, in words chosen carefully when reaction offered quicker satisfaction. It lives in how the house is held—how love is sown, how discipline is shaped, how laughter is protected, and how the Spirit is welcomed in ordinary hours.

A sanctuary forms. A home where Christ reigns as the cornerstone. A community where worship lives in rhythm before it is ever spoken in song. A heritage rooted in sacred habits. Truth buried like seed, destined to awaken through generations.

The builder continues. Harvest may wait beyond his lifetime, but the planting is sure. Though his name may fade from memory, the foundation remains. Legacy sings not through recognition but through permanence.

Heaven seeks nothing grand, only what endures.

Legacy extends well beyond the present moment. When one generation walks upright, the next learns how to stand. A grandchild forms beliefs by observing consistency. A great-grandchild gains wisdom through values passed down at the dinner table and in the way problems are confronted with prayer.

The structures built in quiet faith become shelter to generations who never witnessed the original labor. Prayers once whispered in solitude shape the decisions made decades later. What is planted today remains rooted long after the hands who tilled it are gone. This is the weight of legacy: measured in what endures.

In the hands of the faithful, even the smallest labor can become a lasting legacy.

And through Christ, the work endures.

9

THE UNSHAKEABLE
WARRIOR OF CHRIST

Alife anchored in the Rock of Ages moves with the steadfastness of the Pillars of heaven. Though the winds of chance may howl and the foundations of the earth may shake, such a life shall remain unmoved, for his roots go down into living waters that spring from the very heart of all that exists. Often, it is said that the deepest growth, hidden from mortal sight within the secret chambers of the soul where only the Eye that never sleeps may see, unfolds slowly with grace.

To abide in the fellowship of Christ requires not just fleeting desire but the patient endurance of the earth waiting for spring. It involves being shaped and forged, much like a smith working bright steel in a forge. Standing firm when easy paths tempt with false promises of peace, and continuing on when darkness deepens and no star appears—such endurance is a holy act of resistance against the currents trying to sweep away the children of light. Sand shifts beneath our feet and offers no stable foundation, but stone lasts; on the stone, the wise build their house.

The faith of this nature is not built in joyful gatherings where harpers sing and golden cups are lifted in celebration. It is shaped in dark places, in deep valleys where sorrow dwells, refined through the fires of loss, tempered during long night watches when prayer rises like incense and no answer is received. However, grace sustains what mortal hands cannot endure, and from the depths—like waters emerging from hidden sources—the soul rises renewed.

Thus, the spirit learns to create altars in shadowy valleys, to connect during everyday hours, and to listen to the music of the spheres above worldly noise. Worship feels as natural as breathing, obedience emerges like spring sap, and heaven—aware of all things, big and small—is pleased, even if no earthly witness is present.

The life governed by the deep currents of truth rather than the shifting winds of urgency moves with the rhythm of tides and seasons. Such conviction is strengthened in the silence of waiting, as the tree grows strong in the quiet earth. Forgiveness flows like a river from the mountains, clear, cold, and healing. In stillness, the soul finds its true strength; in the presence of the Eternal, peace falls like dew on the grass. And storms, despite their fury, cannot uproot what has been planted by the hand of the Most High.

Through such lives as these, the Kingdom entrusts its greatest treasures: not merely the work of a day or a season, but the slow shaping of ages. Where others withdraw when the battle grows fierce, these remain; where others scatter their seed upon rocky ground, these plant deep; where the world grows forgetful, these stand as living monuments to the faithfulness that endures.

THE WEIGHT OF PRESENCE

Just as the great trees of the forest contain within their heartwood the memories of many seasons—sun and rain, wind and snow, the slow passage of years—true authority does not come from the noise of trumpet and drum, but from the deep places where the soul has wrestled with truth and been transformed. There is a vast difference between those who wear the appearance of strength, like actors on a stage, and those in whom strength resides as naturally as flame resides within a hearth.

The warrior, unshakeable, understands that influence comes from the Presence that walks with him. This is the mark of those who have traveled long in the paths of the Most High: although they do not speak of their own greatness or send out heralds to announce their arrival, the very air around them becomes charged with power when they draw near. Such weight does not come from charisma that dazzles the eye or from titles given by men, but from the Spirit resting upon them, similar to how the glory-cloud rested upon the Tabernacle in the wilderness.

Without strain, without show, without the clashing of cymbals or the sounding of horns, such a life carries the gravity of the eternal. For this is the way of Kingdom influence: it possesses rather than promotes; it radiates rather than announces. Where the Spirit makes His dwelling, there the very stones remember; holiness shines forth effortlessly, like the moon gives her silver light; and souls are drawn as moths to a flame, not by force but by the beauty of truth made manifest.

Observe how Christ moved among humanity: thirty years in obscurity, learning His earthly father's trade and gaining wisdom and stature quietly in Nazareth; then three years in the spotlight, yet He never sought applause or compromised His purpose for popular approval. His life moved peacefully, like a swan gliding on still waters; His words reflected purity, like goldsmith shaping precious metal; and His presence supported His mission, like pillars holding up a roof. The world, craving genuine substance beneath surface glitter, pursued not fleeting entertainment but true essence.

The eternal truth persists despite the rise and fall of empires and shifting human fashions. A meaningful life isn't created for fleeting applause but for dwelling in the eternal presence of the Most High. It isn't about impressing the crowd but about becoming a sanctuary where the Spirit finds peace. While modern culture emphasizes the visible and immediate, heaven honors the surrendered heart.

In the solitude of the wilderness, strength is forged on the anvil of silence. Words with the power to heal or judge are shaped far from the marketplaces where men buy and sell their voices. Though fakes may fool the eyes of the world for a time, they cannot deceive the gaze of heaven. True presence only comes to the tested and the tried, the humble and obedient—those who have gone into the depths of repentance and come out clothed with righteousness not their own.

True presence moves quietly through the world, needing no one to announce its worth. This is true transformation—not the empty silence of the tomb, but the peaceful quiet of dawn, full of purpose and power. The desire for fame and applause fades away like grass in summer heat; yet the deeper longing persists and grows stronger: to always dwell in the presence of the Beloved, and to become a place worthy of such a guest.

The Spirit of the Living God dwells where ambition is sacrificed on the altar and reduced to ashes. In places where self-exalted towers still reach toward heaven, the anointing lifts like morning mist and leaves. However, where the altar is ignited and the stage is purified, fire comes down—not as a reward for earned merit, but as a sacred trust for future service.

THE MARATHON OF ENDURANCE

A wild flame burns bright and fair, consuming all its fuel in the space of an hour, then dies to cold ash and memory. But the flame that is tended daily with patience and care, fed with the oil of surrender, and trimmed with the scissors of discipline—such a flame endures through the long watches of the night and gives light to many.

True calling reveals itself in the wilderness places where the soul is stripped of all, save its love for the Beloved. Sacrifice speaks its loudest word in the silence where no ear may hear except Him who heareth all things. The finish line belongs to the faithful of heart.

According to the Scripture, the one who endures is honored: David's strength didn't come from his youth's sinews but from deep repentance; Paul's bravery was not based on learned knowledge from human schools but on complete surrender; and Christ's victory was achieved through suffering, much like a grain of wheat falling into the earth and dying to produce abundant fruit. The cross didn't thwart His mission but fulfilled it, and every soul carrying the sacred flame must walk its own Gethsemane—many times, not just once, whenever love demands the laying down of life.

Though the name may fade from people's memories like mist before the morning sun, the impact endures like the mountains do. Seeds planted in hidden places grow long after the sower has moved beyond the circles of the world; admirers disappear like leaves before the autumn wind, but disciples remain like oaks planted by rivers of water. Presence outlives personality just as a song outlives its singer.

Such a life may never win the headlines of the daily scroll, yet heaven keeps careful account in books that shall not perish. Angels draw near when such a soul bends the knee in worship; generations yet unborn are nourished by faithfulness hidden from the eye of the world; and such a life, planted deep in the eternal soil, endures when all the works of pride have crumbled into dust.

Therefore, the flame must be guarded as a treasure more precious than silver or gold. Fed daily with the bread of Scripture; shielded from the winds of distraction that would scatter its brightness; strengthened through the daily offering of the will upon the altar of surrender. Word by word, prayer by prayer, step by step—obedience becomes the oil that feeds the flame, and presence becomes the fire that lights the way.

To finish well means crossing the final threshold with armor scarred from many battles, eyes still fixed upon the face of the King, and fire burning in the marrow of the bones. Heaven does not honor the loudest voice that echoed for a season in the halls of men, but the last warrior standing when the battle is done—the one who bled upon the altar and rose with sword in hand, still ready to serve.

Let the pace slow to the rhythm of eternity; let the voice soften to the whisper of wisdom; let the breath carry the weight of unseen things. When rooms become charged without cause, when words carry weight beyond their sound, may the memory always point heavenward to the One from whom all strength flows.

The warrior was crafted by the hands of the Most High to carry divine presence and to burn with an undimmed flame deep within. Such is the warrior who endures beyond the end of the age; such is the fire that no darkness can extinguish; such is the Kingdom that surpasses every crown that mortal kings may wear.

And now, as the great silence deepens like the hush before the dawn, a stirring begins in the depths. The King draws near with footsteps soft as starlight; preparation transforms into commission; formation blossoms into mission.

10

RISE AND GO

From the depths of stillness, the summons that shakes the pillars of heaven arises; breath gathers like wind before the storm; revelation takes root deep beneath the ribs, where the heart keeps its secrets. The fragile light of morning has been transformed into the settled flame of noon; the tears and trials, the silence and solitude—each moment has become sacred soil from which something greater grows. The hour breathes with the weight of ages, and from the earth, like sap rising in spring, a new beginning starts.

Beyond this threshold lies the long road that winds through many lands, over mountains and moors, through dense forests and vast fields. Knowledge has borne its fruit and become wisdom; revelation has taken flesh and bone; the armor—once worn just for show like a performer's costume—now stands as an extension of covenant blood, forged in the heavens, and tempered in the fires of testing. The King who rescues from the pit now sends His warrior into the battlefield; the fields shimmer beneath the dawn's breath, waiting for those who carry the flame that never dies.

This is the moment when the warrior realizes that his story has always been but a single thread in the Great Tapestry—a Tapestry that was begun before the music of creation first sounded in the void and will continue long after the last star turns cold and falls from the sky like a withered leaf. Every longing he has ever known, like homesickness for a land he's never seen; every battle he's fought, whether with sword in hand or darkness in his heart; every moment he has yearned for something more than the daily sustenance of earth—all these find their meaning at last, like rivers flowing to the sea.

The training described in these pages, the discipline and character and courage—these are but shadows cast by the Reality that stands behind all things. The armor is real, flowing from Christ's armor as light flows from the sun; the strength is absolute, springing from His strength as the branch draws life from the vine; the victory is sure, won by His victory when He strode forth from the tomb with death's keys jangling at His belt.

His name, whispered in a thousand tongues across ten thousand generations, breathed in the last moments of martyrs and sung in the first moments of newborn children, is Jesus. He is the Answer to every question the warrior never knew how to ask, the Home toward which every journey tends, the King of the country for which the warrior has been homesick all his life, though he knew not the name of his heart's desire.

Consider well: every story the warrior has ever loved, every tale of courage and sacrifice and triumph over darkness, has been but a whisper of Christ's story echoing down the corridors of time. Every hero who ever laid down his life for another has been but an echo of the Hero; every king who ever ruled with justice and mercy has been but a shadow of the King.

The dragon is real, ancient, and terrible, but it has been defeated; death is real, cold, and grasping, but it has been conquered; sin is real, black as the pit, but it has been forgiven.

Hell is real, and the Host of heaven has stormed its gates; the curse is real, and the blood of the Lamb has broken it. The story the warrior thought too good to be true—the story of perfect love that casts out fear, of complete forgiveness that washes whiter than snow, of final victory over every darkness that prowls at the edge of the light—this story is Truth itself, the foundation upon which all other truths are built.

And here is the wonder that surpasses even the fairy tales of old: this Story invites the warrior in as a character written into the very heart of the tale, as participant rather than mere reader. The King who conquered death extends His hand, scarred with the nails but warm with life, and says with a voice like the sound of many waters: "Come, follow Me into the places where the light has not yet shone."

The invitation is as simple as a child's trust and as deep as the mystery of redemption: the warrior offers his entire heart, although it is poor and broken, only to find that the King has already given him His heart in return—whole, pure, and ignited with a love that refuses to let him go. He admits that he has tried to be the hero of his small story and failed, but he then sees himself written into the Great Story as a beloved son and brave warrior in the army of the Most High King.

The wind carries more than mere command from the throne of grace; intercession whispers from the roots of ancient oaks, rising like incense from the prayers of all the faithful. Saints and prophets, watchmen and intercessors—all their voices are woven into the music of the spheres, each note precious and remembered. Groans too deep for words, fasts that weaken the flesh but strengthen the spirit, tears that water the ground of faith—all are recorded in the books of heaven, and legacy rises into motion at last.

So rise.

The summons now sounds with the voice of the archangel's trumpet. The hour moves forward like an unstoppable tide. Rise in the Name that is above every name, the Name that overcame death, hell, and the grave. Rise with blood stirred by holy fire, like steel tempered in the forges of the Almighty, forged for the conquest of darkness with the cross burned deeply into the metal of the soul. Rise with righteousness as a compass needle pointing true north, and the Kingdom of heaven as the destination that will not fail.

Heaven itself leans near, and the eyes of angels gaze upon the earth with expectation bright as starlight. Thrones stir with the weight of glory yet to be revealed; the voice of the King sounds with the deep thunder of purpose ancient as the mountains, rolling through the high halls of eternity—never with haste, for He who dwells in eternity is not bound by the tick of mortal time.

Establish the altars where none have stood. Consecrate the ground that sin has poisoned. Rebuild the ancient ruins, the devastations of many generations. Awaken the sleepers who have slumbered overlong. Anoint the chosen ones for the work prepared beforehand. Declare liberty to the captives and the opening of prison doors. Illuminate the dark places where hope has guttered low.

The King walks beside his warrior, just as a friend would walk with a friend along the road. Although the gap between the Sovereign and the servant remains as vast as the space between the stars and the earth, His love bridges every distance. The road stretches farther than the eye can see, winding through both good and bad times.

Mountain ridges stand in quiet anticipation, ready to hold new altars where worship may rise; old strongholds tremble at the footfall of righteousness, feeling their foundations shift as the ground itself is reshaped by holy purpose.

A charge resounds across the waste places of the world, echoing from the throne room of heaven to the farthest shores of mortal lands: Advance in the name of Christ the King, the Lord of lords, the Prince of Peace! Let every footfall carry the weight of divine purpose; let every breath declare allegiance to the One whose reign shall have no end.

Trumpets now sound on the horizon, their loud call echoing like thunder through the highlands where sentinels hold watch. Flags are raised—worn from numerous battles, bloodstained from heroes, yet still carrying the emblem of promise and the fire of loyalty that endures. Altars reignite beneath hands strengthened by resolve, where cold ashes once lay forgotten during years of exile.

This is the moment of holy resolve where the heart chooses the narrow path even if the entire world chooses the broad one. March forward under the banner of righteousness. Continue with the strength of His Spirit, who raised Christ from the dead; proclaim freedom where chains have held their captives; plant truth in soil where lies have taken root and produced bitter fruit.

Go forth, beloved warrior. May the Living Water of Yahweh cover you. May the Power of the Holy Spirit and the Blood of Jesus Christ divinely protect you always. For Christ who died. By Christ who rose. Through Christ who reigns. To the glory of Christ, whose Kingdom shall endure always and forever.

APPENDIX

THE BROTHERHOOD OF
BIBLICAL WARRIORS

These are the stories of men who answered the call. A few without certainty, yet all of them with surrender. Men who wrestled fear, doubt, and failure, then stepped into fire regardless. Their strength was found outside themselves—within their resolve to trust the One who called.

Some began in obscurity, others in palaces. Some heard the call in prayer's silence, others in battle's heat. Each journey was unique, yet every man placed his faith in the Lord. Each life became a vessel through which God displayed that His power transcends a man's past and transforms his weakness. A blemished history glorifies the Lord even more when surrendered to Him—His glory shines brightest when the trials He delivers His children from are truly formidable.

Through these chosen figures, heaven touched earth. Idols shattered. Kingdoms trembled. Giants fell. Altars rose. The proud were humbled, the broken restored. In every story, glory belonged to God who moved through each man.

These lives were preserved for imitation over admiration. They awaken the reader to true faith. The same God who called them still calls. The same Spirit who filled them still empowers. The same mission awaits men of Christ willing to answer.

MICHAEL THE ARCHANGEL: THE ORIGINAL WARRIOR OF CHRIST

Long before nations fell, before Eden's soil knew the bitter taste of sin, war stirred in glory's heights. Rebellion first rose from heaven's own blazing light. In the very halls where perfection dwelt, pride dared bloom like a poisonous flower, bringing the first terrible fracture to eternity's untainted harmony.

Satan—once robed in splendor beyond mortal comprehension, adorned with wisdom that made the sages appear as children, crowned with music that set the very stars to dancing—sought a throne that was never his to claim. "I will ascend," the fallen one declared in words that would echo through all the ages of the world. "I will raise my throne above the stars of God ... I will make myself like the Most High" (Isaiah 14:13–14). Thus did the unthinkable unfold: mutiny in the very courts of the Most Holy, treason against the throne of Christ before time began.

Heaven itself trembled beneath the weight of such treachery. The Book of Revelation speaks of a great red dragon whose tail swept a third of the stars from their courses—those bright angels who, deceived by Lucifer's golden lies, fell with him into the abyss (Revelation 12:4). Light that had known neither shadow nor stain was twisted into darkness. Beauty that had never known blemish became blasphemy incarnate.

Then Michael stood—the first warrior to take up arms for the glory of Christ.

Like thunder before the storm, the great prince rose to defend his Lord's honor. Here was born the very essence of what it means to be a warrior of Christ: absolute allegiance to the throne of grace, unwavering defense of divine sovereignty, with righteous fury against all that would usurp the King's rightful place.

Obedience needed neither herald, explanation, nor moment's hesitation. Heaven's commander lifted himself to action, and his very name, "Who is like God?" became the battle cry of all who would fight for Christ, a sword drawn against any arrogance that dared blaspheme an answer to this eternal question.

Michael became the first to understand that true warfare concerns neither personal glory nor the pursuit of fame, but instead concerns itself with defending the honor of the King. In him was forged the original pattern: the warrior who fights for Christ alone, who draws strength from his Master's authority rather than his own might, who wields his sword in love for the one true King rather than in anger.

Then war was unleashed in the high places in its most terrible form. "And there was war in heaven," the ancient words proclaim. "Michael and his angels fought against the dragon, and the dragon and his angels fought back. Yet he was neither strong enough, and they lost their place in heaven" (Revelation 12:7–8).

This was the first great battle for Christ's supremacy, and Michael led the charge with zeal. The dragon fell like lightning from heaven's pinnacle (Luke 10:18), cast down from realms of light to prowl in darkness. Satan, once heaven's brightest jewel, became earth's cursed exile. Wings that had been clothed in worship were singed by the fires of justice. And faithful Michael, the original warrior of Christ, led the charge that drove back the first assault against the throne of grace.

Still does Michael's warfare continue in realms unseen, for he remains the eternal champion of Christ's Kingdom. The great archangel stands as sentinel and guardian, the original defender still defending, still fighting for his beloved King. In the visions granted to Daniel, Michael appears as "the great prince who protects your people" (Daniel 12:1).

Even now, in this very hour, the first warrior contends in those high and hidden places where angels resist the encroaching darkness for the sake of the King's beloved.

Thus does Michael's legacy speak to all who would take up the warrior's calling: he remains the pattern, the prototype, the first of those who fight for Christ. His allegiance teaches us that true strength comes from surrender to the King. His victory shows us that no enemy can stand against those who fight in Christ's name. His faithfulness reminds us that the battle belongs to the Lord.

ABRAHAM: THE WARRIOR OF OBEDIENT FAITH

From Ur of the Chaldeans, Abraham ventured forth from a cradle of ancient splendor where towers and ziggurats reached like grasping fingers toward heaven. In shadowed halls, priests whispered their secrets to Nanna, the moon god, and the wisdom of empires gleamed like fool's gold.

Into the shadowed magnificence came a voice clear and direct from the throne of heaven itself: "Go from your country and your kindred and your father's house to the land I will show you" (Genesis 12:1).

Here was the first great call to arms in the war of faith, the first summons to abandon the seen for the unseen, the first command to choose the foolishness of God over the wisdom of men.

Into Canaan he wandered, a land soaked in blood and spiritual abominations, where the people offered their children to Baal's hungry fires. The very air reeked with the smoke of unholy sacrifice. Yet Abraham, first soldier in the army of the One True God, planted his standard in defiled ground and built altars of a different kind, to worship the living Father whose voice had called him from afar.

Initially known as Abram, meaning "exalted father," though the irony ran deep, for no child's laughter echoed in his tent. Sarah, his wife, was as beautiful as the dawn but as barren as winter stone. One star-filled night, the Lord drew His faithful soldier beneath the swirling constellations and said: "Look toward heaven, and number the stars, if you are able to number them ... Such shall your offspring be" (Genesis 15:5).

Against all evidence, against all reason, against the testimony of empty years and his wife Sarah's closed womb, Abraham dared to believe the impossible. And the chronicler of heaven wrote these words which echo still: "And he believed the Lord, and he counted it to him as righteousness" (Genesis 15:6).

Years wheeled by like seasons in an endless winter. The womb remained sealed, the promise apparently sleeping. Yet the word of the Lord stood firm as mountain stone. Then came the day when God renamed His warrior: Abram became Abraham—"father of many nations"—while Sarai became Sarah, "princess," for kings would spring from her laughter yet to come (Genesis 17:5, 15–16). New names carved into flesh and soul, sealed by covenant, written by heaven's own breath. The first warrior of faith bore new colors into battle.

Still they wandered and worshipped and waited, until war itself came hammering at their tent door.

Like wolves descending from the mountains, a confederation of eastern kings swept down through Canaan with fire and sword. Cities crumbled before their advance. Blood ran crimson in the valleys. In the chaos and slaughter, Lot, Abraham's nephew, was taken captive and carried away like spoils of war. When word reached the patriarch, he did not hesitate, calculate odds, or count costs.

Abraham rose like thunder before the storm. Here was warfare of a different kind—the patient battle against doubt, yet the swift strike of righteous fury. Three hundred and eighteen men, trained in his own household, followed their commander into the night. Under the cold fire of stars, by strategy born of covenant and courage forged in faith, Abraham struck like the very hammer of God. The patriarch shattered the pride of kings, pursued them beyond Dan to Hobah, and brought back his kinsman from the jaws of captivity.

Yet even in victory, the warrior faced his subtlest test.

The defeated king of Sodom, who should have knelt in gratitude, dared instead to bargain with the man who had delivered him. Spoils of war were offered like honeyed poison: gold and garments, honor and riches. Abraham would not be bought with the world's coin. "I have lifted my hand to the Lord God Most High," he declared, "I would take neither a thread nor a sandal strap nor anything which is yours" (Genesis 14:22–23). No earthly king would claim credit for what God alone had wrought.

Then, from the mists of mystery, came another king entirely: Melchizedek, priest of the God Most High, ruler of Salem, the peaceful. He emerged as conqueror yet as one who stood between heaven and earth, bearing neither sword nor spoil yet bread and wine—simple elements pregnant with eternal meaning. No lineage is recorded for this figure, no genealogy traced, no beginning or end declared. He appears in Scripture like a divine signature written in starlight, blessing Abraham with words which carried the weight of eternity: "Blessed be Abram by God Most High, Possessor of heaven and earth" (Genesis 14:19).

In the brief, blazing encounter, the veil between worlds grew thin. Abraham glimpsed a priesthood bound by neither earthly law nor tribal lineage, yet something older, higher, eternal. Something which whispered of the One who would come to bless yet to bear the weight of sin itself—"a priest forever after the order of Melchizedek" (Psalm 110:4). The warrior of faith recognized his Commander's shadow and bowed, giving tithes by neither command yet by the deep recognition of the heart.

Yet the Lord's final test for His chosen warrior still waited on the heights of Mount Moriah.

The promised child had come at last. Isaac—laughter itself given flesh, born from Sarah's aged womb when hope had withered to a thread. The miracle they had waited for through decades of delay now walked beside his father, carrying wood for the sacrifice, innocent as the morning. Then came the Voice again, terrible in its simplicity:

"Take your son, your only son Isaac, whom you love, and go to the land of Moriah, and offer him there as a burnt offering" (Genesis 22:2).

Here was the ultimate warfare of faith—against visible enemies yet against the deepest loves of the human heart. In faithful obedience that defied every instinct of flesh and blood, Abraham took his beloved son and climbed toward the place of sacrifice. The old man believed the God who had given life to the barren womb could raise even the dead

(Hebrews 11:19). His hand trembled with agonizing reverence as he raised the blade above his only son—and then the Voice which had called him from Ur spoke once more:

"Do neither lay your hand on the boy nor do anything to him, for now I know you fear God" (Genesis 22:12). A ram appeared with its horns caught in the thicket, a substitute, sacrifice, and sign.

Because Abraham passed this final test of warfare—the battle between love and obedience, between the seen and the unseen—the Lord confirmed His covenant with an oath: "Because you have done this and have neither withheld your son, your only son, I will surely bless you … and in your offspring shall all the nations of the earth be blessed" (Genesis 22:16–18).

This is why the Lord chose Abraham to be the first warrior of faith. Neither for strength of arm nor keenness of blade. Neither for worldly wisdom nor flawless virtue. But because Abraham would train his household in the ways of righteousness (Genesis 18:19). Because when the ultimate test came, he would lay even the fruit of God's promise back upon the altar in complete surrender.

Abraham built no lasting cities. Abraham wrote no codes of law. Yet from Abraham's line came the chosen nation of God's people, Israel. From this nation arose a King. From the King flowed salvation for all the world.

Abraham forsook everything to follow a heavenly whisper. He waited decades for one promised son and offered him in total obedience, so much so that it overwhelmed the angels. The world still shudders under the impact of Abraham's "yes"—his first major victory in the war of faith, and the initial triumph of a warrior's heart fully surrendered to God's will.

MOSES: GOD'S WARRIOR AGAINST THE GODS OF EGYPT

Egypt was a realm of ancient pride and deeper bondage. From dawn to dusk, Egyptians bowed before deceiving gods—each claiming dominion over mortal life, each promising prosperity which turned to dust, protection crumbling like sand, and peace hollow as broken reeds. A land gorged with false shrines and false altars yet starving for truth.

Into this house of bondage came Israel's children from famine's grasp, seeking survival in foreign soil. They settled and thrived in Goshen—fruitful, strong, multiplying as the ancient promise spoken to Abraham beneath the stars. Years passed, names forgotten, favor transformed to fear. A new king rose over Egypt, knowing neither Israel's forefathers nor its God. Suspicion hardened into policy, which in turn hardened into oppression as cruel as a winter wind.

Taskmasters rose with whips and chains. Upon bleeding backs were built Pithom and Pi-Ramesses—monuments to Egypt's arrogance, raised by Hebrew hands crying to heaven for deliverance.

At this time, Pharaoh decreed death for every newborn son of Israel, commanding that they be cast into the very river that preserves the land. Throughout four hundred years: the people groaned beneath their burden, yet above every lash, every stifled cry, every prayer seeming to vanish into empty air, the God of Abraham watched. He waited. He prepared His champion.

When Pharaoh's decree rang like a funeral bell, Levi's tribe dared defy the tyrant's word. Three months hiding their son, muffling his cries from prowling soldiers. When concealment became impossible, the mother wove a basket of bulrushes, sealed with pitch and prayer, placing it among the Nile's reeds, casting upon the mercy of the God who sees all.

Pharaoh's daughter came to bathe in sacred waters. She discovered the basket, heard the infant's cry, and her heart moved to compassion. She named him Moses, meaning "drawn out of water," and the future deliverer grew up inside the very palace of his people's oppressor. Hebrew by blood yet schooled in enemy halls.

Moses grew in rank and favor, trained in all Egypt's wisdom until mighty in words and deeds. Yet the memory of his true people remained somewhere in either his conscious or subconscious mind. Witnessing an Egyptian striking a Hebrew slave, Abraham's blood stirred within him like fire. Moses struck down the oppressor, burying the body in sand.

Murder, even in righteous fury, makes a poor foundation for deliverance. The next day, when Moses sought to make peace between two Hebrews, one turned on him: "Who made you prince and judge over us? Do you mean to kill me as you killed the Egyptian?" The deed was now known. Pharaoh sought Moses, and the prince became an exile, trading palace halls for desert silence.

In Midian's wilderness, Moses fled, far from the granite courts of his youth. Forty long years passed like wind across empty places while heaven shaped its chosen instrument. Moses married, tended flocks belonging to another, spoke little of his haunted past. Desert's vastness humbled what Egypt's grandeur had inflated. While Moses waited in obscurity, learning hard lessons of patience and dependence, heaven remained faithful to ancient promises.

Then came the day when everything changed. Fire appeared within a bush, the flames consumed nothing and burned as bright as God's glory while leaving every leaf untouched. Moses turned aside to behold this wonder, and from the fire's heart came a voice: "I am the God of your father, the God of Abraham, Isaac, and Jacob ... I have surely seen my people's affliction in Egypt ... Come, I will send you to Pharaoh."

Moses trembled like a leaf in a storm. "Who am I to go to Pharaoh?" he stammered, overwhelmed by failures, a trembling tongue, and forty years of exile.

"I will be with your mouth," the Lord promised, "and teach you what you shall speak."

The exile returned to face the empire that had cast him out.

Upon arrival, Moses was taken before Pharaoh. Yet he stood with Aaron his brother, appointed by God to be his voice, and behind them both stood the invisible presence of the Almighty. Together, they entered the court of the earth's mightiest empire, bearing a message which shook the foundations: "Thus says the Lord, the God of Israel: Let my people go."

Words fell like thunderbolts in halls of idols. Pharaoh's heart remained stone.

God issued a sign—a challenge hurled at Egypt's gods and the throne upholding them. Aaron cast down his staff before Pharaoh and his court. Wood became a living serpent, writhing with divine power. Egypt's wise men and sorcerers attempted to match this wonder; their staffs also became serpents—as if the kingdom of lies could mimic the voice of truth. For a moment, the contest seemed equal.

Aaron's serpent was then charged with the Almighty's breath and devoured all the others.

This was a cosmic duel of sovereignties. Egypt's gods were summoned and quickly revealed to be inferior. The Most High had spoken His challenge. Egypt had been warned.

Then began the great plague war between heaven and the house of bondage.

The sacred Nile turned to blood, leaving Osiris, the god of life, unable to keep the river pure. Frogs infested the land, ridiculing Heket, the goddess of fertility. Gnats emerged from the dust as Geb, the lord of earth, watched helplessly. Swarms of flies overtook cities, and Beelzebub was powerless to stop them. Thousands of livestock died while Hathor and Apis, protectors of cattle, watched every beast perish. Boils broke out on skin while gods of healing, Sekhmet and Imhotep, were struck silent.

Hail fell mixed with fire, and Nut, sky goddess, gave no shelter. Locusts devoured what remained while Min, god of harvest, watched his realm become desolation. Darkness swallowed even Ra, the sun god, for three days.

Finally came the tenth blow. In one night, Death walked throughout Egypt claiming every firstborn—from Pharaoh's heir to the slave girl's child. The destroyer passed over houses marked with lamb's blood alone, a foreshadowing symbol of the Lamb to be slain for all of salvation.

Upon these plagues, the Lord's people were released in a moment of agony after Pharaoh had lost his firstborn. They began their journey home. And even while followed in vengeful pursuit by Egyptian chariots while crossing the Red Sea, the Lord waged war again for His beloved people.

The Egyptian army was swallowed entirely and drowned at the bottom of the sea after the Hebrews had safely made it across the divinely parted waters, split apart by God Himself with perfect precision and timing. The chariots of the devoured army cry out from the depths to this day.

Each act was a sword thrust into Egypt's spiritual core. What the empire trusted, God overturned. What they worshiped, God wounded. What they exalted, God cast down.

And the instrument of this cosmic victory? A murderer who had fled in shame. A stuttering exile who doubted his own voice. A broken shepherd who had once tried to deliver Israel by his own strength and failed utterly. Now Moses stood clothed in the Lord's authority and watched an empire crumble.

God chose Moses for obedience rather than eloquence, for willingness rather than worthiness. Through this unlikely champion, the Almighty humbled earth's mightiest nation. Through Moses, God reminded every generation of His fight for His people, the destruction of false gods, and His delight in using weak vessels for great works.

Moses stood before kings with knocking knees. Yet the Lord of Hosts stood with Moses, and this made all the difference.

When the battle concluded, Egypt was left shattered amid its lost pride. Israel was liberated under the desert stars, singing hymns of salvation. It was solely by the Lord's mighty right hand—who often confounds the wise by choosing the foolish and shames the strong through the weak—that victory was achieved.

Moses the murderer became Moses the deliverer. Moses the exile became Moses the lawgiver. Moses the stammerer became the voice through which God spoke judgment upon empires and deliverance to the oppressed.

JOSHUA: THE COMMANDER WHO CARRIED THE PRESENCE

In the shadow of Egyptian bondage arose Joshua. Ephraim's son drew first breath when Pharaoh ruled with an iron heart and Israel groaned under the taskmaster's lash. From those affliction furnaces would emerge a warrior whose faithfulness would echo through ages.

Joshua served as Moses's attendant before heaven called him to command. He waited—patient as stone, faithful as sunrise. In the Tent of Meeting, Joshua lingered at the Divine presence's threshold. There, in sacred space between earth and heaven, he was forged. Quietly. Steadily. In the great prophet's shadow, Joshua's strength took root like cedar planted by flowing streams.

When it was time for the test, Joshua was prepared.

Command's first challenge arose at Rephidim when an ancient enemy attacked unexpectedly. The Amalekites—descendants of Esau's grandson, harboring deep-seated hatred against God's chosen—rushed down from the desert like lightning. These were no ordinary raiders seeking plunder; they targeted the vulnerable members of Israel's wilderness journey. This event served as a test of Joshua's leadership and a spiritual battle, resonating through history.

Moses positioned himself upon the hilltop with God's rod in his hands, while Joshua led the fighting men below into the valley of conflict. As long as the prophet's hands remained raised toward heaven in prayer, Joshua and his warriors succeeded; when Moses's arms grew tired and started to fall, Amalek gained the upper hand. Aaron supported Moses's arms until sunset, and Israel achieved a complete victory.

Here Joshua learned the great lesson to define his life: victory comes through alignment with heaven's will, through battles fought on knees as much as with blade and shield. Physical warfare was the visible expression of spiritual conflict, and success depended entirely on maintaining a connection with the source of all strength.

This lesson would prove invaluable in trials ahead. Years later, as the nation stood trembling at promise's threshold, Joshua was chosen as one of twelve to spy out the land heaven had sworn to give them. For forty days they explored its regions—valleys rich with grain and honey, hills crowned with vineyards, rivers running clear and cold. Canaan was also a fortress. Its cities rose behind massive walls, its warriors trained from childhood in war's arts, its high places reeked with altar smoke where innocent blood was spilled to gods whose very names were curses.

The Canaanites were a confederation of ancient tribes: the Amorites, with pride reaching to the sky; the Hittites, whose chariots thundered across the plains; the Jebusites, who fortified mountain strongholds; and the Perizzites, living in unwalled towns with hearts as hard as stone. Their gods—Baal, the storm-rider; Molech, the child-devourer; and Ashtoreth, queen of abominations—were carved into every hill and worshipped through rituals that defiled both body and soul. This was not just an empty wilderness waiting to be claimed but a battleground where darkness had taken deep root for generations.

Ten spies even saw giants residing in the area and lost courage. Their report spread panic through the camp like wildfire: "We are as grasshoppers in their eyes," they mourned. "The people are stronger than we are." The nation's resolve melted away like wax before fire. Meanwhile, Joshua remained steadfast, like a mountain planted by the Divine hand.

"If the Lord delights in us," he declared, "He will bring us into this land and give it to us ... Fear them no longer! Their protection has departed from them; the Lord stands with us." Though the people took up stones to silence him and Caleb, though the very air crackled with rebellion, Joshua refused to recant his faith. Heaven itself intervened, and because of their unbelief, God declared none of the doubting generation would enter the promised land. Joshua and Caleb alone would remain.

Joshua waited. Through forty long years he wandered beside the disobedient, buried those who had chosen fear over faith, and trained a new generation who had never known Egypt's chains. When Moses's time came to its appointed end, the mantle passed—from prophet to warrior, from one who had spoken with God face to face to one who would carry His presence across Jordan's waters.

"Take Joshua the son of Nun," God commanded, "a man in whom dwells My Spirit, and lay your hand upon him." Moses died upon Mount Nebo with eyes undimmed and strength unabated, and God Himself buried the great lawgiver in a valley known to no mortal man. Leadership passed to one who had carried presence, endured testing, and refused to break when people bent like reeds before every wind.

Joshua's commission was to obey rather than innovate, to follow rather than forge new paths.

"Be strong and courageous," the Lord commanded His chosen warrior. "Let this Book of the Law never depart from your mouth; meditate on it day and night, which you may be careful to do all written therein. Then you shall make your way prosperous, and then you shall have good success."

Jericho stood before them like a challenge carved in stone—an ancient fortress of the earth, a city that could withstand the rise and fall of empires. Its massive walls resembled cliffs, with gates secured by iron, and its defenders ready for siege and battle. Heaven provided a strategy unlike any mortal scheme. Over six days, Israel marched quietly around the city—only the Ark of the Covenant and ram's horn blasts marking their path. On the seventh day, they circled seven times, then shouted aloud, causing the earth's foundations to shake. When the people shouted, the wall collapsed flat, allowing everyone to storm into the city, each man directly before him, and they seized the city.

Joshua's hand touched no stone until obedience was complete. Victory belonged to the Almighty's presence, triumph to the God who fights for His people.

City after city fell before Israel's advancing armies. Thirty-one kings in total bowed necks to Joshua's sword. Joshua led with reverence rather than revolution. Commander in flesh yet steward of something far greater. He never sought glory for himself; he consistently carried out the Lord's command as Moses received it on the mountain, wrapped in fire and cloud.

When Joshua's days drew toward their close like shadows lengthening toward evening, he gathered Israel's leaders for one final charge.

He spoke of victories won and promises kept, of land flowing with milk and honey now stretching beneath their feet. Then he gave them a choice every generation must face: "Choose this day whom you will serve … As for me and my house, we will serve the Lord."

Joshua died at the age of one hundred and ten, full of days and honor. They buried him in Ephraim's hill country, near the inheritance he had helped secure for his people. "Israel served the Lord all the days of Joshua, and all the days of the elders who outlived Joshua."

Joshua led with the sword yet lived by the Word. He inherited nothing that he had first refused to obey. He carried out everything God commanded, trusted when the path seemed strange, waited when others rushed toward disaster, stood firm when people shook like leaves in a storm. Because of this faithfulness, land found rest—peace born of promise fulfilled and covenant kept.

Joshua was faithful as sunrise, constant as the northern star. When heaven needed man to carry its presence into the promised land, it chose Joshua.

His obedience banner still flies. His patient example of faithfulness still beckons. Joshua blazed a trail every Christ warrior must walk: from servanthood to leadership, from human wisdom to divine command, from seen to unseen, trusting always in the God who keeps His promises.

The faithful sword calls all warriors forward. Promise's conquest continues.

CALEB: THE OLD MAN WITH A YOUNG HEART

Walking alongside Joshua's faithful sword was another figure whose story burns with a different passion—someone who carried the sacred fire for forty-five years of trial, watching it grow brighter. Caleb, unlike others, came from a foreign land, not from the promise's lineage. He was born a Kenizzite among the ancient peoples dwelling in Canaan's hill country since time began, descending from proud Canaanite clans with roots as deep as mountain cedars. However, through faith's mysterious transformation and steadfast loyalty, he was grafted into God's people, his foreign blood turned into covenant gold. His life stands as a testament: covenant loyalty surpasses birthright, and heaven's adoption goes beyond any earthly inheritance.

When twelve spies had first beheld Canaan's abundance—valleys flowing with grain and honey, vineyards heavy with purple clusters, cities whose walls rose like mountain cliffs—Caleb had stood with Joshua as twin voices crying against fear's flood.

Ten of the spies returned with trembling reports of giants whose stature reached toward heaven and fortress walls built by titan hands, declaring: "We cannot ascend against this people, for they are mightier than we." Yet Caleb's voice rang clear: "Let us go up at once and possess the land, for we are well able to overcome it."

This unwavering trust had earned heaven's promise, to stand among the sole survivors of his generation who would enter their inheritance when the time of testing was complete. Through the long wilderness years, Caleb had kept vigil over hope itself. He buried companions whose courage had crumbled beneath desert trials, watched beloved faces fade like flowers in drought, and mourned an entire generation choosing present safety over eternal promise. Divine word burned in his breast like an altar flame, which adversity served only to purify and strengthen.

As conquered Canaan stretched before them like a tapestry woven from prophecy turned into reality, Joshua prepared for the great division of tribal inheritances. Caleb stepped forward— the young scout transformed into a patriarch whose snowy beard reflected wisdom earned in sorrow's furnace, and whose eagle eyes still burned with unquenched fire drawn from wells deeper than mortal years.

"Behold, this day I am eighty-five years old," he declared before an assembly like thunder rolling across mountain peaks. "As my strength was then in youth's bright morning, even now remains my strength for war in age's golden evening … Give me this mountain, whereof the Lord spake in the ancient day when promises were young and giants seemed unconquerable."

Caleb set his heart upon the divinely and personally promised Hebron— a mountain stronghold still held by the very Anakim whose dreadful reputation had once turned Israel's courage to water and sent ten spies fleeing like startled deer. The fortress which had bred terror into hearts of the Hebrew reconnaissance was the very prize Caleb had treasured through decades of faithful endurance, polishing vision until it shone like burnished gold.

By sword and strength, Hebron became his portion. At fourscore years and five, with vigor undimmed by time's passage and sinews strengthened by heaven's favor, he drove out giants who had haunted a generation's dreams like shadows from primordial darkness. Cities that once inspired dread crumbled before faith clothed in righteous action. His body had been preserved because his spirit had remained unshaken through his crucible years. Every syllable of heaven's promise found earthly fulfillment.

Where Joshua conquered nations through strategy and divine obedience, Caleb waged war against time itself—proving that sacred vigor belongs to a faithful heart regardless of mortal years. His fire burned with endurance rather than spectacle, with steady devotion rather than brilliant display, constant as the northern star guiding wanderers home. He sought heaven's fulfillment above earthly recognition. When vindication dawned at last, he ascended his mountain with strength renewed.

Caleb's chronicle lives in accomplished deeds rather than written words, in persistent faithfulness rather than celebrated victories. His life became living proof: faith expresses itself through sustained choice rather than momentary feeling, through decades of constancy rather than fleeting enthusiasm. True obedience outlasts the grave itself. Age refines rather than weakens those whose hearts choose eternal promise over visible circumstance.

Hebron belonged to Caleb because Caleb had belonged entirely to God through forty-five years of tested loyalty.

The flame that burns faithfully endures forever, kindled by divine breath and fueled by covenant wood. The mountain still calls to those who trust in heaven's timing through seasons of testing, then rise to claim what the Almighty has sworn with oaths as unbreakable as starry courses.

EHUD: THE LEFT-HANDED DELIVERER

Darkness brooded over the promised land like storm clouds gathering before a deluge. Israel groaned beneath Moab's iron yoke, necks bent beneath foreign mastery. The Moabites were descendants of Lot through his eldest daughter. Distant kin by blood, bitter enemies by choice, they had grown mighty in the harsh steppes where survival demanded cruelty. Idolaters by heritage, conquerors by ambition, they bowed before Chemosh the destroyer and delighted in subjugation like wolves savoring a fresh kill.

Allied with Ammon and Amalek, tribal heathens born of rebellion, they had swept westward across Jordan like a plague wind, emboldened by numbers and Israel's apostasy. Eighteen years they ruled with unchecked arrogance, grinding beneath their heel the people once freed from Egypt's furnaces.

Even then, the Lord remembered His covenant children. From Benjamin's tribe, smallest of Jacob's sons yet fierce as the mountain lion, the Almighty raised a deliverer whose strength lay in surprise rather than symmetry.

Ehud was his name, and his sword hand was his left.

In those days, left-handedness carried a burden of social scorn and superstitious mistrust. The right hand embodied all blessings: strength, honor, divine favor flowing down through generations like golden streams. It was a hand of covenant promises and priestly benedictions, of royal power and warrior's glory carved in stone and song.

The Left bore darker associations: weakness, deception, ill fortune whispered in the marketplace and council hall. Even the Hebrew tongue betrayed this bias, for *śemō'l* (left) shared roots with words meaning "dark" and "unlucky".

Warriors throughout the ancient world trained exclusively to face right-handed foes. Combat stances, defensive positions, weapon place-ment—all assumed that the enemy's blade would strike from their right side like lightning from a clear sky. Guards inspected left hips where right-handed men wore swords, never suspecting the right thigh, where a left-handed assassin might conceal his fang like a serpent hiding beneath rose petals.

Greatest irony dwelt in his tribe's very name. Benjamin meant "Son of the Right Hand"—Jacob's favored designation for his youngest son, blessed above his brothers. Yet from this people of the blessed right hand, God raised a left-handed deliverer. Divine providence delights in such reversals, confounding human wisdom through unexpected strategy like a master craftsman working with broken tools to forge a masterpiece.

What others dismissed as deformity, the Almighty had forged as deliverance.

Ehud fashioned a dagger double-edged and short enough to vanish beneath a tribute-bearer's robes like a secret wrapped in silk. He bound this blade against his right thigh—the one place where guards would never search, for who expects left-handed man to reach across his body for death's cold kiss?

He carried Israel's tribute to Eglon, king of Moab—a man grown corpulent on Israel's submission, so vast he ruled through terror more than strategy. He was an obese mountain of flesh crowned with cruel ambition. His court glittered with plundered gold from conquered cities, walls hung with tapestries woven by enslaved hands, floors paved with stones torn from Israel's altars.

Most galling, Eglon had established his throne in the City of Palms, within Jericho's ancient walls. This was Israel's former place of triumph, transformed into a monument of shame. Insult cut deeper than sword wounds, festering like poison in a covenant heart.

When tribute was delivered and delegates dismissed, Ehud returned as if struck by divine inspiration. "I have a secret message for you, O king," he declared with a voice smooth as honey concealing steel. Eglon dismissed his guards with a wave of his jeweled hand. The upper chamber was cool, carved high above the court like an eagle's nest, a place of luxury and false security where tyrants dream of permanence while kingdoms crumble beneath them.

Irony burned like fire in dry grass: Israel's victory had become Moab's throne.

"I have a message from God for you," Ehud whispered. In one fluid motion, he stepped forward, reached across his body with a hand that the world scorned, and drew his concealed blade. Before the king could cry out or flesh could flinch, Ehud drove the dagger deep into Eglon's belly. The hilt vanished after the blade, swallowed by folds of flesh like a stone sinking into deep water.

Ehud locked the chamber doors and vanished while confusion spread.

Ehud escaped to Seirah's rocky fortress, then ascended Ephraim's peaks. There, he blew a ram's horn, sounding a call to arms like a trumpet, awakening courage through valleys which summoned the Hebrews home.

Israel rose as one people from the cave and the threshing floor. Men stirred like bears from winter sleep, seized buried swords grown hungry for justice, and gathered to Ehud's banner. The yoke was broken with a single stroke of a hidden blade. With God's unlikely assassin leading, they marched to Jordan's fords, where fleeing soldiers would attempt to escape like rats from a burning granary.

The scattered Moabite forces were thrown into chaos. Their king was slain, their leadership broken, and their hold on Israel was slipping away. They fled toward the river like leaves blown by a hurricane, but none reached safety. Ten thousand soldiers fell—"all strong and able-bodied men," warriors in body but lacking divine favor, slaughtered like grain cut down by a righteous reaper.

This was a decisive judgment rather than just a minor conflict, a divine ruling inscribed in blood and steel. The Lord raised a man whom the world would not notice, turning what society saw as weakness into a strategic advantage, much like a skilled blacksmith forging gold from scrap. Through this unlikely vessel, oppressors crumbled like towers built on unstable ground. Jericho was regained as if recovering treasure from thieves. The land—scarred, haunted, and long restless like a stormy sea—was granted peace for eighty years, like a tired traveler finding shade under a large oak.

Ehud's chronicle embodies an eternal principle carved in heaven's foundation stones: the Almighty chooses weak things of the world to shame the strong; He chooses the despised to overthrow the mighty.

His left-handedness symbolizes how every human limitation can be turned into a divine opportunity, how what seems like a disadvantage can be reshaped by providence into a decisive victory.

Faithfulness sharpens every blade, redeems every weakness into strength. In the sovereign hand of Most High, even the scorned and overlooked become mighty deliverers, proving that heaven's ways transcend earth's wisdom like stars outshine candle flames in midnight's depth.

GIDEON: THE FEARFUL MAN CALLED MIGHTY

The age of judges had dawned over Israel. Gone were the days of Moses's unified leadership and Joshua's conquering armies. Without a king or central authority, each tribe pursued whatever seemed right in its own eyes, caught in an endless cycle of rebellion, judgment, repentance, and rescue.

This pattern would define generations: Israel would abandon the Lord, embracing Canaanite idolatries. Divine protection would withdraw, leaving them vulnerable to waiting enemies. Oppression would follow until the people cried out in desperation. Then, in unfailing mercy, the Lord would raise up a deliverer—a judge—to break the chains of bondage. Yet within a generation, the cycle would begin anew.

After Joshua's death and the passing of those elders who had witnessed the conquest of Canaan, the people abandoned the Lord's covenant. They forgot His sacred promises, bowed before Canaanite Baals, and adopted the corrupt practices of surrounding nations. As in every generation since Eden's Fall, spiritual rebellion opened the gates to political bondage.

This time, judgment was delivered by a formidable alliance: the Midianites allied with the Amalekites and eastern tribes to create a confederation of terror. These warriors aimed for plunder and formed a coordinated military force excelling in economic warfare. They had what Israel lacked—large herds of camels that transported warriors over hundreds of miles at unparalleled speeds.

Each year, with military precision, this desert coalition would sweep across the Jordan's waters just as Israel's crops ripened. Like an irresistible plague of locusts, they would devour every green thing, slaughter livestock, steal what they could carry, then vanish back into the wilderness before resistance could form. For seven bitter years this devastation continued, reducing Abraham's descendants to hiding in mountain caves like hunted animals (Judges 6:1–6).

The promised land had become a landscape of terror. Israel cried out to heaven.

Gideon, son of Joash, was threshing wheat when the angel found him. He labored not upon the traditional threshing floor, but within a winepress, hiding his work from prowling Midianite patrols. This was no mighty warrior preparing for battle. Here worked as a frightened farmer grinding grain in fearful solitude, embodying the reduced state of God's chosen people.

Into this scene stepped the angel of the Lord, speaking words appearing to mock the circumstances: "The Lord is with you, mighty warrior".

Mighty warrior? The title rang hollow in Gideon's ears. If the Lord was truly with him, where were the miracles their fathers had recounted? "Pardon me, my lord," he stammered, "if the Lord is with us, why has all this happened to us?" When the divine call came to save Israel from Midian, Gideon could only protest his weakness: "How can I save Israel? My clan is the weakest in Manasseh, and I am the least in my family" (Judges 6:15).

Such was the man's transparent honesty. Gideon possessed no military training, commanded no army, harbored no strategy. Only uncertainty dwelt within his spirit. Yet the Lord offered no rebuke. "I will be with you," came the divine promise, "and you will strike down all the Midianites".

Still, Gideon hesitated. He requested a sign, and fire rose from the solid rock to consume his offering. Even then, his doubt persisted. Gideon spread a fleece on the threshing floor: "If you will save Israel by my hand, let the fleece be wet with dew while the ground remains dry" (Judges 6:37). Dawn revealed his request was granted. Yet, doubt still haunted him, and he tested heaven's patience again: "This time let the fleece be dry while the ground is covered with dew". Once more, the Lord replied—patiently, mercifully, without rebuke.

For the Almighty does not scorn the hesitant heart, He walks beside it through the valley of fear.

When battle's hour dawned, Gideon's call brought thirty-two thousand men—respectable numbers, though still vastly outnumbered. Yet the Lord declared even this army too large. "You have too many men. I cannot deliver Midian into their hands, or Israel would boast, 'My own strength has saved me.'" Twenty-two thousand fearful souls were dismissed. Another test reduced their numbers to three hundred. These warriors were chosen for strength, for vigilance and faithfulness.

They carried weapons defying earthly sense: fragile clay jars concealing torches, ram's horns for trumpets, empty hands where swords should rest. No armor protected them, no shields guarded their lives.

Under the cover of darkness, they silently moved into position overlooking Jezreel Valley, where the large Midianite army rested beneath swirling stars. At Gideon's signal, jars breaking to unleash sudden torchlight, trumpets echoing through the quiet night—three hundred voices united in proclaiming: "A sword for the Lord and for Gideon!"

The enemy camp erupted in chaos. Roused by blazing lights and phantom trumpets appearing to come from every direction, confused by darkness and echoing war cries, the Midianites turned weapons upon one another in terror. They fled in panic as Israel's victory unfolded as a gift through surrender, rather than seizing it through strength (Judges 7:16–22).

Gideon's story highlights consecration over confidence. He started as one hiding in shadows, a questioner trembling before divine calling. Yet when heaven spoke, Gideon listened. When uncertainty threatened to paralyze, he tested God's word with honest doubt. He trembled through preparation, questioning every command and seeking confirmation for each promise.

Then, when the moment called for action, when obedience mattered more than understanding, Gideon stepped forward and obeyed. Through faith, no matter how reluctant or mixed with human weakness, victories are received as gifts rather than earned as wages.

The fleece was never meant as a formula for future generations; instead, it stands as a testimony to how gently the Lord speaks to uncertain hearts. The Almighty does not punish the fearful, He strengthens them for the work ahead. He shapes warriors from winepresses, transforms cowards into champions, calls forward the least likely, and makes them brave beyond imagining.

For across the centuries, the Lord still whispers to every reluctant heart: "The Lord is with you, mighty warrior."

JEPHTHAH: THE OUTCAST WHO RETURNED WITH FIRE

East of Jordan, Gilead's hills bore witness to a birth wrapped in shame. The child's father was Gilead himself, a man of standing and substance. His mother, unnamed in Scripture and unwelcome at the hearth, was a harlot. "You shall inherit nothing in our father's house," his legitimate brothers declared with cruelty, "for you are the son of another woman" (Judges 11:2).

Jephthah fled eastward into the rugged wilderness of Tob, beyond the reach of Gilead's elders and their righteous disdain. There, in harsh country, the unexpected began to unfold. Men gathered to him, outcasts like himself, the desperate and discarded whom Scripture calls "worthless fellows" (Judges 11:3). These were outlaws and fugitives, souls with broken names and severed futures, men whom respectable society had cast aside like refuse.

Why did they follow this rejected son into the wasteland? Because they recognized in him what they yearned to become. In him, they glimpsed the ability to command without title, to speak with authority though never invited to council tables. His leadership emerged as naturally as water from a spring, as if heaven had chosen him while earth spurned him.

Under his banner, these misfits found belonging, direction, and protection. They became his brotherhood, following him into danger and returning with victory's spoils. In the wilderness wastes, he forged what Gilead had denied him: a tribe bound by loyalty rather than blood, crowned with grit rather than gold, called by necessity rather than birthright.

Though he knew it little, the Lord was already preparing him for greater deeds—to lead far more than a few outcasts when the hour of testing came.

The hour dawned when the Ammonites stirred beyond the Arnon River like wolves scenting weakness. These were distant kin to Israel, descendants of Lot through his younger daughter, yet hostile in heart and hardened by generations of idolatry. Though once spared by divine command during Israel's wilderness wandering, they now rose with grievances born of twisted memory and deliberate falsehood (Deuteronomy 2:19). They laid claim to Gilead's borderlands, accusing Israel of ancient theft, demanding territory they insisted had been stolen from their fathers.

Yet their claim was a lie.

The disputed territory had never belonged to Ammon's crown. It had once been ruled by Sihon, king of the Amorites, a Canaanite warlord who had seized the land from Moab before Israel ever approached those borders. When Israel's wandering generation asked Sihon for peaceful passage, he answered with war's fury. Israel defended themselves and prevailed by the Lord's mighty hand, taking possession of

Amorite territory through righteous conquest (Numbers 21:21–26).

Generations later, the Ammonites deliberately blurred these distinctions, exploiting the similarity between "Amorite" and "Ammonite," hoping that time had dulled memory and historical truth could be rewritten. This was ambition cloaked in deception, a blade sheathed in false righteousness.

When Gilead's elders found themselves pressed by this eastern threat, they swallowed their pride and sought the man they had rejected. To Jephthah they came with entreaties and promises, begging him to lead their armies. The irony cut deep, those who had declared him unworthy of inheritance now deemed him worthy of dying for their cause.

Yet he possessed what they desperately needed: knowledge of the covenant and Israel's sacred history. Though raised in exile, far from priest and temple, he had forgotten nothing of the chronicles entrusted to his people. The wilderness years, the conquest of the Amorites, the Lord's commands—these were a living record, preserved and passed down with intentional care.

When Ammon's king made false claims, Jephthah responded clearly and effectively. Using diplomatic tactics, he presented a message based on historical facts and covenant law (Judges 11:14–27). He stated that Israel had asked for peaceful passage through Edom and Moab during their exodus, but these requests were denied. Similarly, when they asked Sihon the Amorite, he attacked without reason. Israel defeated him through divine help and seized the Amorite lands—territory that had never belonged to Ammon.

Further, for three hundred years, Israel had dwelt in those cities without challenge. "Why did you make no attempt to reclaim them then?" he demanded. Finally, he placed the matter before the ultimate tribunal: "I have done you no wrong, yet you would make war against me. Let the Lord judge between us this day" (Judges 11:27).

This was the response of a man who knew his people's history and trusted his God—speaking with covenant authority despite his illegitimate birth.

The Spirit of the Lord came upon him with power (Judges 11:29). From Gilead through Manasseh he marched, gathering Israel's forces for the decisive confrontation. At Mizpah, in a moment which would haunt the ages, he made his fatal error.

Driven by human desperation, Jephthah spoke a vow heaven had never required: "If You deliver the Ammonites into my hand, then whatever comes from the doors of my house to greet me upon my return shall belong to the Lord, and I will offer it as a burnt offering" (Judges 11:30–31).

Why did he bind himself with such reckless words? Perhaps fear clung to him despite divine empowerment. Perhaps the desperation of one too long overlooked drove him to seek assurance beyond what God had already promised. The surrounding nations practiced child sacrifice on their unholy altars—abominations the Lord had explicitly forbidden Israel (Deuteronomy 12:31).

Yet in his zeal to prove devotion, he took it upon himself to make a covenant with God that God had never asked him to make in the first place.

Victory came swiftly. The Ammonites fell before Israel's advance, their false claims shattered like pottery against stone. The land trembled with deliverance's joy. Yet when the conquering hero returned home, triumph turned to tragedy in a single heartbeat.

From his threshold came neither servant nor beast, his daughter— his only child—dancing with tambourine and song, celebrating her father's return with innocent joy (Judges 11:34). The covenant's terrible weight crashed down upon him. He tore his garments in anguish, for the words vowed in falsely perceived desperation had become a sword through his own soul.

She asked for time—two months to wander the mountains and mourn her virginity, the future which would never unfold, the children she would never bear (Judges 11:37). Then she returned, ready to fulfill her father's pledge with courage which shamed the earth and broke the heart of heaven.

Scripture speaks with haunting restraint: "He did to her according to his vow" (Judges 11:39). No altar is described, no flames detailed.

A judge empowered by God's Spirit had fallen prey to his own mouth's rashness. He had made a vow the Lord never requested, offered what heaven never desired. For the God of Israel had already declared His will with unmistakable clarity: child sacrifice was an abomination, never divinely commanded (Jeremiah 7:31). The same God who stayed Abraham's hand and condemned Molech's altars delights in obedience rather than blood.

Yet in his understanding, breaking a vow to God seemed a greater evil than spilling his daughter's blood. Hence, he chose the unthinkable, transforming devotion into destruction.

His name is famously recorded in faith's eternal record, reminding us that God uses imperfect vessels, where both bravery and tragedy can coexist in the same heart (Hebrews 11:32). He trusted in divine salvation and led bravely. However, in his desire to demonstrate his devotion, he crossed into madness that God's law explicitly forbade. The Spirit had already strengthened him, and victory was certain. The vow was more harmful than needed—it was a desperate deal with a God who grants freely to those who trust Him.

His daughter endures Israel's yearly lament—four days each year when young women remember the one who died for a father's reckless words rather than a nation's sins (Judges 11:40). Her name remains unrecorded, but her sacrifice is never forgotten.

The outcast judge reminds every warrior that the Lord requires humble trust rather than reckless pledges. His promises rest on divine mercy; human desperation finds no place here. When we attempt to bargain with heaven through unnecessary vows, we risk building false altars to grief rather than glory.

Obedience surpasses sacrifice. Wisdom exceeds zeal. The fire he kindled was never requested. The vow he made was never required. The daughter he sacrificed was never his to offer.

The lesson burns clear across the centuries: attempt to make no deals with God except those He has already asked you to make.

SAMSON: DIVINE STRENGTH WITH IMPERFECT WILLPOWER

The days of Samson occurred near the twilight of the judges' era. Israel drifted aimlessly through a spiritual wilderness, lacking a king or unity, with walls too weak to keep out any compromise.

For forty years, the Philistines controlled the promised land. From their five coastal cities, these sea warriors built an empire of iron chariots and bronze spears, asserting dominance through bloodshed. Out of such a time was born a judge destined to resist, a man raised for war in a generation that had forgotten how to fight.

Covenant gift rather than natural endowment provided his strength, a manifestation of the Spirit's power, never reward for personal righteousness. Set apart from birth as a Nazirite by divine decree, he grew tall in Zorah on Dan's frontier, where Israel's hills bowed toward the Philistine plain. There, in such borderland between compromise and calling, the Spirit of the Lord first began to stir within him (Judges 13:25).

Divine favor flowed because the Almighty had chosen to work through such an unlikely vessel. When the Spirit rushed upon him, he tore apart a lion with his bare hands as easily as rending cloth (Judges 14:6). In Ashkelon's streets, he struck down thirty warriors. Foxes became living torches in his hands, sent through enemy fields like agents of divine wrath. When delivered bound to his foes at Lehi, the cords melted from his arms like flax before flame, and with a donkey's jawbone he felled a thousand men (Judges 15:14–15). None could match his might, for it was never his own.

Though he judged Israel for twenty years, he led it away from righteousness rather than toward her divine calling. Forbidden women captured his heart, unclean things drew his touch, sacred fire became his plaything. The Nazirite vow marking his calling meant little to the life he lived. Though set apart by heaven, his heart remained unsubmitted. Though filled with supernatural power, he lacked spiritual purity. His strength endured through countless compromises while his soul withered.

Then came Delilah, bringing more danger than any army he had faced.

Flattery replaced fury in her arsenal, silver where others had wielded steel. The Philistine lords promised her wealth if she could uncover the secret of his impossible strength. Day by day, she pressed him with words softer than silk yet sharper than any blade. What his enemies could never touch through force, his own flesh began to weaken to through desire.

"Tell me, wherein lies your great strength?" she whispered (Judges 16:6). He answered with arrogant mockery: "If they bind me with seven fresh bowstrings ..." The binding occurred while he slept, then came her cry, "The Philistines are upon you!" Yet he snapped the cords like scorched threads.

Again, she pleaded. Again, he deceived: "If they bind me with new ropes ..." Once more, she attempted betrayal. Once more, he rose in power, the trap proving useless.

A third time she pressed him. "If you weave the seven locks of my hair into the loom ..." She accomplished the weaving while he slumbered. Again, she raised the alarm. Again, he awoke in strength, tearing free.

Three betrayals. Three escapes. No apology from Delilah's lips, no repentance in her heart. Only her relentless persistence and his spiritual blindness. Samson knew she meant to destroy him. He knew his enemies planted her. Yet he remained in her embrace as the noose tightened, whether from arrogance or addiction to his own destruction. His strength and resilience had become his gods.

Day after day, she wore him down "until his soul was vexed unto death" (Judges 16:16). Eventually, he surrendered—more out of exhaustion than love. "No razor has ever touched my head," he admitted, "for I have been a Nazirite unto God from my mother's womb" (Judges 16:17). The secret was now exposed.

While he slept in her lap, the razors came. The locks fell like autumn leaves. The outward sign of inward consecration was severed.

The Lord departed from him.

He awoke to fight as before, expecting the familiar surge of might. Instead, heaven remained silent. No power flowed through his limbs. The Philistines seized him, tore out his eyes, dragged him in chains to Gaza—the very city whose gates he had once carried upon his shoulders. There he ground grain in his enemies' house, broken and brought low.

In the silence of such shame, transformation began.

Scripture records with understated power: "Yet the hair of his head began to grow again" (Judges 16:22). This detail transcended mere observation—it carried signal and sign. Though the covenant had been trampled, it had never been erased. Though the man had failed, the calling had never been revoked. Now, grinding grain in humiliation, the broken champion began to remember who he truly was.

His captors brought him to Dagon's temple to provide amusement for Philistine nobility. Above him, the massive roof groaned under the weight of thousands: rulers and generals, nobles and revelers, all gathered to celebrate their triumph and mock the God he represented. Yet in the shadow of those mighty pillars, he accomplished what he had rarely done in all his years of supernatural strength.

He prayed.

"O Lord God, remember me, and strengthen me only this once" (Judges 16:28). Neither for personal glory nor conquest. Neither to win favor nor settle scores. For the first time, he asked to be faithful rather than great. Nothing remained to prove, nothing left to lose. In such emptiness, he made his first true offering: complete surrender.

Heaven answered.

Placing his hands upon the stone pillars, he leaned into surrender with all the weight of his returning strength. The pillars tumbled. The roof collapsed with the thunder of divine judgment. The temple fell upon the heads of kings and captains alike. "The dead which he slew at his death were more than they which he slew in his life" (Judges 16:30).

He fell, neither in vanity nor lust nor pride, which had marked his earlier victories.

He fell in obedience, and such distinction made all the difference.

His life remains a tapestry of contradiction: chosen yet reckless, empowered yet ungoverned, mighty yet undisciplined. Still the Almighty used him—through divine sovereignty rather than human consistency. His final act was an expression of surrender rather than a display of strength. His last breath held more genuine faith than all his previous battles combined.

Such an offering proved sufficient.

For the Lord rewards repentance rather than perfection. Even the broken may be mended. Even the fallen may finish faithful.

This hope echoes through his story: no failure proves final; no stumble lies beyond grace's reach. True strength manifests through the presence of God in a humbled heart rather than the absence of weakness. The warrior of Christ must only remember who gives him breath and therefore return to the altar of surrender.

For the God who called forth strength in Zorah still calls men today. The same Spirit who stirred the champion now searches the earth for willing hearts.

SAUL: THE ANOINTED WHO FELL

The age of judges was nearing its final hours. For countless generations, Israel had only known leaders raised in times of crisis—judges who delivered during oppressions, prophets who conveyed the Lord's words, priests who lit sacred fires on ancient altars. Here, theocracy existed alongside monarchies, a nation ruled by unseen divine authority while surrounded by visible crowns. The repetitive cycle of rebellion, oppression, and deliverance that defined the era of the judges was now giving way to what the people believed would bring stability: the demand for an earthly king.

All around them, the kingdoms of earth boasted golden scepters and iron armies. Egypt loomed like a brooding giant to the south. Philistines pressed westward with sea-born might. Ammon, Moab, Edom, and Aram encircled the promised land, each led by kings who ruled through sword and tribute. Israel stood outnumbered and often outmatched, bearing God's promises while feeling the weight of earthly pressure.

In the face of foreign banners and battlefield splendor, the tribes grew restless with divine rule. They longed for the visible strength other nations displayed, the tangible power they could see and follow into war. "Give us a king to judge us like all the nations," they demanded of Samuel the prophet (1 Samuel 8:5).

Security they truly craved rather than mere kingship—a crown they could see, a warrior they could follow, a throne granting them the appearance of might. In making this request, they rejected the One who had brought them through the wilderness, parted seas before their feet, and toppled the walls of Jericho. Their petition was granted, though heaven issued a solemn warning.

The Almighty chose a king from among the tribes, and the age of monarchy began.

From Benjamin's inheritance came one named Saul, son of Kish—a man of noble bearing who stood head and shoulders above his countrymen (1 Samuel 9:2). Handsome and strong, marked by a humble spirit appearing to shrink from greatness rather than grasp for it. While searching for his father's lost donkeys in the hill country, he stumbled instead into the path of destiny.

The aged prophet Samuel anointed him with sacred oil, kissed him with the kiss of covenant, and declared with prophetic authority: "Has the Lord anointed you to be prince over His inheritance?" (1 Samuel 10:1). The Spirit of God rushed upon him like a mighty wind. A new heart was given, transformed and empowered for the throne awaiting.

For a season, divine favor rested upon him.

War became his proving ground and victory his constant companion. The Ammonites fell before his advance. Moab, Edom, and the kings of Zobah trembled at his approach. The ancient curse of Amalek was broken beneath his sword. Even the mighty Philistines retreated from his banner (1 Samuel 14:47–48). Wherever he turned his face in battle, triumph followed. Every engagement ended in Israel's favor while his reign flourished. The nation, long fractured and uncertain, stood united behind a crown for the first time in her history.

Even as success mounted like an altar of victories, a shadow began to grow within the king's heart. The man who towered above others in stature proved diminished in the measure mattering most—obedience to heaven's voice.

At Gilgal, when Samuel delayed and the people grew restless, Saul usurped the priest's sacred role and offered sacrifice with unauthorized hands (1 Samuel 13:8–14). At Amalek, when commanded to destroy utterly the cursed nation, he spared what God had devoted to destruction, keeping the choicest spoils and the enemy king alive (1 Samuel 15:9–23). Time and again, he chose appearances over allegiance, expedient outcomes over faithful obedience, the preservation of his reputation over surrender to divine will. The voice of the people grew louder in his ears than the voice of the Lord. The crown, having once rested lightly upon his brow, grew heavy with the weight of self-will.

The Lord expressed his sorrow over making Saul king, saying, "I regret having made Saul king," because he has turned away from following Me and disobeyed My commands (1 Samuel 15:11). Though still on his throne, the Spirit's empowerment had left him.

From this moment, his descent was as swift as his rise had been glorious. The throne received in genuine humility became an object of desperate clinging. Jealousy consumed his peace as young David's fame grew. Rage replaced wisdom when prophets spoke unwelcome truth. Forbidden mediums became his counselors when heaven's voice fell silent. The warrior who had once led Israel to unprecedented victory became a man at war with God's own anointed successor. What had begun as a divine calling dissolved into madness.

Even in his tragic fall, courage remained. At Mount Gilboa, surrounded by Philistine forces and pierced with arrows, he chose the dignity of death over the disgrace of capture. "Draw your sword and thrust me through," he commanded his armor-bearer with final authority. When his servant refused to touch the Lord's anointed, Saul fell upon his own blade. With him fell his sons, his dynasty, and Israel's first experiment with earthly kingship (1 Samuel 31:3–6).

His life stands as a solemn warning: divine anointing provides little armor against the arrows of pride. A calling unguarded by obedience will always collapse beneath the weight of self-will. He reminds every warrior of the greatest threat lying often within—the ego seeking to usurp God's throne in the heart.

The Spirit of the Most High had rested upon him. The Kingdom had been his to steward in righteousness. When the self took the seat belonging to the Almighty alone, downfall became inevitable.

The same God who removed his crown continues to work redemption in humble hearts. Though pride led him to ruin, the Lord's mercy remains for any who will bow beneath the mighty hand of heaven.

The crown belongs to the humble. The Kingdom belongs to the obedient. The victory belongs to the Lord alone.

DAVID: THE WARRIOR-KING AFTER GOD'S OWN HEART

In Bethlehem's quiet hills, where shepherds had watched their flocks since Abraham's time, the future king of Israel drew his first breath. These were the twilight years of the judges, when the old covenant ways were yielding to earthly monarchy. Samuel the prophet, bearing the weight of Saul's failure, came seeking one who might restore what had been lost to a nation crying out for visible strength.

When the prophet arrived to announce Israel's next ruler, the youngest son of Jesse remained in the fields while his brothers stood before the man of God. One by one, Jesse's sons presented themselves— each strong, each bearing the look of warriors, each seeming fit to lead armies. None found favor in heaven's eyes. Only when all had passed did Samuel ask, "Are these all your sons?" Only then was the shepherd summoned, ruddy from sun and wind, still carrying the scent of his flock (1 Samuel 16:11).

The youth came bearing only a heart which pulsed with love for the

God of his fathers. Heaven's voice rang clear: "Arise and anoint him, for this is the one" (1 Samuel 16:12). Sacred oil flowed over his young head, and destiny was declared in this humble house.

Yet the crown would wait.

His rise began in Elah's valley, where Israel's armies faced the Philistine war machine. For forty days their champion giant Goliath had issued his challenge, and for forty days Israel's courage had withered.

Although Goliath's stature was intimidating to the Hebrew army, it was dwarfed by the zeal of young David for his God and his people.

"You come to me with sword and spear and javelin," he declared as he ran toward the giant, "I come to you in the name of the Lord of hosts, the God of the armies of Israel" (1 Samuel 17:45). One stone from his sling felled the Philistine giant. One prayer moved two armies. In that moment, Israel saw what kingship could become when combined with genuine faith.

Over the years, the triumphs of David slowly awakened darkness in Saul's heart. The troubled king heard the women's songs, "Saul has slain his thousands, and David his tens of thousands."

The shepherd who had delivered Israel as a boy became a hunted fugitive, learning lessons no palace could teach in the caves of Adullam and the wilderness of Judah.

There, the broken and desperate gathered around David like the warrior Jephthah—men crushed by debt, outlaws fleeing justice, souls wounded in the long wars. Under his leadership, they became different, warriors bound through shared exile and common hope rather than tribal loyalty. In those harsh wilderness years, David learned to depend utterly on God's provision, to find strength in weakness, to lead through service rather than command.

Saul's life was in his grasp twice, and both times he chose to spare the king who wanted him dead. "I will not raise my hand against the Lord's anointed," he whispered, even when the chance arose (1 Samuel 24:10). This restraint showed a heart that caught heaven's attention. This heart revered God more than man and trusted divine timing over human opportunity.

When dark news came from Mount Gilboa—saying Saul and Jonathan had fallen before Philistine arrows, David tore his garments and composed a lament destined to outlive empires: "How are the mighty fallen" (2 Samuel 1:25). Though the throne lay vacant, his heart remained bowed before the sovereignty of the Most High.

The ascent to full kingship tested both patience and character. Seven years passed before the northern tribes joined Judah in acknowledging him as king. In his thirtieth year, he seized Jerusalem—the unconquered Jebusite fortress destined to become the city of David. There he brought the Ark of the Covenant, processed with dancing and songs, making ancient stones sing with joy.

In his prime, David's kingdom extended from Egypt's border to the Euphrates. The Philistines were defeated, Damascus paid tribute, and the wealth of nations flowed through Jerusalem's gates. He became more than a conqueror; he was a poet king, writing psalms that voiced every human heart. "The Lord is my shepherd, I shall not want" flowed from his pen, which comforts souls across the ages (Psalm 23:1).

Yet at power's peak came his greatest downfall. When kings traditionally led armies into battle, he stayed behind in Jerusalem's comfort. From the palace rooftop, he saw Bathsheba bathing, and desire overpowered the restraint that had once saved Saul's life. Adultery led to deception, deception demanded blood, and Uriah the Hittite—whose loyalty embarrassed his king—died by royal order to hide sin born of idleness. The shepherd who once ran toward giants now fled from his conscience's voice. Victory in every battle had led to defeat in the secret chambers of the heart.

When Nathan the prophet confronted him with the parable of the stolen lamb, David neither hid nor made excuses. The facade of the righteous king crumbled as recognition dawned. "I have sinned against the Lord," he confessed with broken honesty (2 Samuel 12:13). From anguish came Psalm 51: "Create in me a clean heart, O God, and renew a right spirit within me."

The sword never departed from his house afterward. His children rebelled, his throne shook, yet through every trial, his heart turned again to the altar of surrender. His psalms became the language of every soul that has known both triumph and tragedy, teaching the world that godliness lies in the willingness to return to grace rather than in perfection.

David died with blood on his hands, yet mercy was granted to the faithful monarch. Through David's descendants would emerge the true King, Jesus Christ, the Son of God, who will reign from earthly Jerusalem and from heaven's throne forever.

His life mirrors every believer's journey from the initial calling, through failure, and into restoration. David remains the eternal reminder that God seeks faithful hearts rather than flawless performance. Genuine greatness lies in never ceasing to pursue the face of God.

BENAIAH: THE PRIEST-WARRIOR OF COVENANT AND FLAME

From Levi's ancient house came one whose name would echo in the councils of kings and live in the songs of warriors. Benaiah, son of Jehoiada, was born in the sacred space between altar and battlefield, where sacrifice meets steel and holy silence gives way to righteous storm. His youth passed beneath the tabernacle's shadows, where incense rose like prayers while distant hammers rang upon iron. When his hour came, the man stepped forth—neither singer of psalms nor seeker of renown—as a blade drawn from heaven's own scabbard.

In Moab's blood-drenched plains his legend began. There, the warrior met two champions such as the world rarely breeds, "lionlike men of Moab," Scripture names them with the restraint of one who has witnessed wonders (1 Chronicles 11:22).

These Ariels bore the fierce aspect of beasts and the terrible countenance of those who serve dark powers. Perhaps they were descended from the Emim of old, those giants who once walked those hills before Lot's sons drove them into shadow (Deuteronomy 2:10–11). They stood as champions of the pagan god Chemosh, and their very presence was affront to the God of Israel. With no herald to proclaim the deed and no minstrel waiting to weave the tale, Benaiah faced them in the fearsome silence of the wilderness. They fell before the priest's son, who was blessed divinely gifted martial prowess.

More challenges lay ahead. When winter enveloped the land and snow coated the hills, the warrior descended into a pit where a lion had sought shelter from the storm. No one called him to this act—only the voice that speaks to hearts trained in righteousness guided him. Benaiah ventured into the frozen darkness, risking death, while wiser men might have closed the opening and left. When he emerged, the mighty lion was still, and only the winter wind witnessed what true courage looks like when no audience is present except heaven.

From the south came his greatest challenge, an Egyptian warrior of ancient and fearsome kind. "A man of great stature, five cubits high," is written in the chronicles—a giant nearly touching eight feet tall in his sandaled height (1 Chronicles 11:23). The spear in his mighty grip was "like a weaver's beam," the very phrase used once to describe Goliath's weapon (1 Samuel 17:7).

Here was no ordinary soldier; a champion of the old fallen blood stood before Benaiah, his bronze armor engraved with images of Egypt's gods—the hawk and serpent, the sun and scythe. In his presence, the giant embodied all the pride of the ancient kingdom that once held Abraham's descendants in chains.

Against this living monument of earthly power, the son of the priest poetically carried a shepherd's staff. What followed was less of a battle and more of a judgment—quick, certain, and final. The giant's own spear became the tool of his downfall, pride's weapon turned into heaven's rod. Thus Egypt, which had once been swallowed by the sea, was humbled again by someone who served the God of Israel.

These were deliberate acts of bravery, shaping a man in fires that burn away impurities. The tests confirmed the metal's true strength.

David, familiar with the hearts of men as a shepherd with his flock, appointed Benaiah to oversee the Kerethites and Pelethites—foreign warriors serving as the inner guard of the throne (2 Samuel 8:18). These fighters, coming from distant lands, were as fierce as winter wolves and as loyal as hounds. They followed the priest's son because they perceived in him an innate authority, something that commands without speech, leading simply through his example of what a man should be.

When David's days drew toward their close and the question of succession cast shadows over the kingdom, Benaiah's faithfulness shone brightest. While Adonijah reached with grasping hands for a crown which was never his to take, the captain rode with Nathan the prophet and Zadok the priest to Gihon's ancient spring, where Solomon received the anointing heaven had decreed (1 Kings 1:38–39). Through all the storm which followed, Benaiah remained what the warrior had always been—unmoved, unswayed, constant as the northern star.

When peace required the edge of justice, the new king turned to his most trusted blade to rid the kingdom of those who sought the downfall of the Lord's anointed.

Joab was the first to be slain by Benaiah for Solomon, the blood-stained general who had killed noblemen during acts of friendship. Now, the traitor clung to the altar's horns, hoping the sacred bronze would protect the deeds done by unworthy hands. But Benaiah entered the sanctuary with a clarity that recognized mercy unacknowledged becomes unavoidable judgment. Following Solomon's command, the sword delivered its final blow to someone who had prioritized personal ambition over loyalty to his king (1 Kings 2:28–34).

Adonijah followed, the prince unaware that kingships are anointed from above. His request for his father David's servant girl Abishag seemed innocent; however, he knew that taking the woman of a king was to claim his throne altogether. Solomon viewed his brother's bold move as treasonous. Benaiah's subsequent actions on the king's behalf were swift and deadly (1 Kings 2:25).

Then Shimei, who had cursed David during his moment of greatest sorrow, defied the oath of mercy and his vow to stay within Jerusalem's walls by crossing the Kidron. Despite the promise to remain loyal, his old hatred overpowered prudence. This act marked the turning point of justice, leading to the final cleansing of the house from those who sought to defile it (1 Kings 2:44–46).

For these faithful services, striking only when righteousness demanded, serving truth rather than personal will, Solomon raised Benaiah to command all the armies of Israel (1 Kings 2:35). The mantle which Joab had stained with innocent blood now rested on shoulders bearing no such burden.

Yet power did not truly change the man, for Benaiah had learned early on that real strength is neither in the roar of lions nor in the obedience of lambs. His was the fierce gentleness of those who understand that the sword's purpose is to serve divine justice, not to satisfy the cravings of ambitious hearts.

Through all the years which followed, his name became byword for the kind of man kings pray heaven will send them: one who fears God more than death, who serves righteousness above reward, who will descend into whatever darkness duty demands. In the great scroll of Scripture his deeds shine like stars: the descent into the pit, the slaying of giants, the faithful guardianship of thrones.

JEHU: THE BATTLE-HARDENED AVENGER OF IDOLATRY

Israel's kingdom, torn from David's house by Jeroboam's revolt a century before, had wandered long through rebellion's wilderness. When Solomon's golden age ended and the realm split in two, the northern tribes had fashioned their own religion of convenience—two golden calves erected in Bethel and Dan to sever the people from Jerusalem's temple and prevent pilgrimage to Judah's rival kingdom. These idols stood as spiritual shortcuts, allowing Israel to claim Yahweh's name while avoiding His presence.

Over the generations, the Omride dynasty had established itself through military prowess and foreign alliances, yet with worldly success came spiritual compromise. Then came Ahab, and with him, darkness took dominion.

Through marriage to Jezebel, the Sidonian princess whose father,

Ethbaal, ruled both Tyre and Sidon, paganism gained a foothold in Israel's high places. This alliance brought wealth and security against Damascus, though at a catastrophic price. Jezebel reshaped the nation's soul, importing Phoenician religious practices of sacred prostitution and child sacrifice. Yahweh's prophets were hunted and slaughtered. Holy altars were torn down. The Lord's name was traded for Asherah groves and Baal temples reeking with the smoke of abominations.

Even fire summoned from heaven on Mount Carmel could not eradicate the spiritual cancer. When Elijah's flames consumed the sacrifice and the false prophets, it appeared that light had broken through. Yet Jezebel's throne persisted, her altars remained, and darkness gradually returned.

When a house's iniquity reaches its appointed measure, divine judgment comes riding. Thus, the Lord of Hosts raised up Jehu, drawn from the dust and blood of Israel's frontier wars rather than palace courts.

He was neither priest, scholar, nor diplomat, but a chariot commander hardened by years of warfare against Hazael's Syrian forces, unknown to palace intrigue while intimate with sword and shield. At Ramoth-Gilead—the contested fortress city east of Jordan where Israel and Damascus had spilled blood for generations—a young prophet arrived bearing oil and a commission to shake kingdoms.

Sacred oil flowed over his battle-scarred head while heaven's charge rang in his ears: "Rise and strike down the house of Ahab. Avenge the blood of my servants the prophets. Cleanse the land of its defilement" (2 Kings 9:6–7). No ceremony followed, no coronation with a golden crown. Only God's word and a storm set loose upon the earth.

He mounted his war chariot and drove with such fury toward Jezreel, the royal winter residence where Ahab's palace overlooked the fertile valley. The watchmen upon the walls declared, "The driving is like the son of Nimshi, for he drives like one possessed" (2 Kings 9:20).

The sons of King Ahab, Joram and Ahaziah, rode out to meet this approaching tempest. Jehu's message cut through diplomatic niceties: "What peace can there be while the whoredoms and witchcrafts of your mother Jezebel continue?" Jehu's bow sang, the arrow found its mark, and Joram fell pierced through the heart in the very field once belonging to Naboth. Ahaziah attempted flight, yet judgment followed like hunting hounds. Two kings fell in a single day.

When Jehu's chariot rolled through Jezreel's gates, one figure remained defiant. From her high window Jezebel looked down, arrayed in royal robes as if earthly splendor could shield her from heaven's wrath. "Is it peace, Zimri?" she called with venomous mockery, invoking an ancient regicide's name.

Jehu answered with stark simplicity. Looking up to where palace eunuchs watched from the casement, he spoke three words which would echo through the ages: "Throw her down."

They did.

She fell from the heights of her own making. Blood painted the walls, her body was trampled beneath the hooves of horses that had once carried her in triumph. When they came to bury what remained, they found only fragments—skull and feet and palms, for the dogs had devoured the rest, fulfilling Elijah's prophecy (1 Kings 21:23).

At Jezreel, Jehu's commission expanded beyond heaven's original charge. He slaughtered seventy sons of Ahab, executed the royal officials, and butchered the priests of Baal—acts which, while fulfilling prophecy, were carried out with an excess and ruthlessness revealing the darkness growing in his own heart.

The valley, which should have witnessed surgical judgment, became a charnel house where divine command and human ambition mingled like blood and mud.

From Jezreel, the purge persisted. Disguised as religious fervor, Jehu gathered all the priests and prophets of Baal to their temple. "Ahab served Baal only a little," he declared with deadly irony, "Jehu will serve him much." The temple quickly filled with eager worshipers until it was full. Then, the doors were closed, and the deadly slaughter began. No one escaped. Altars were destroyed, sacred stones crushed into dust, and Baal's temple was turned into what Scripture describes as "a latrine unto this day" (2 Kings 10:27).

Zeal had ridden forth. Vengeance had been satisfied.

Yet here, triumph turns to tragedy, as Jehu's story, which started with divine fire, concludes in the ashes of only partial surrender.

The man who had torn down Baal's abominations with righteous fervor proved strangely blind to idolatries serving his own purposes. While he purged Jezebel's priesthood and reduced foreign temples to rubble, he carefully preserved the golden calves in Bethel and Dan, the ancient snares Jeroboam had crafted to maintain independence from Jerusalem's authority. To walk fully in the Lord's law would have required centralizing worship at Jerusalem's temple, meaning the end of the northern kingdom's political independence. Jehu was willing to serve heaven when it aligned with his political interests, yet when obedience would have cost him his throne, he chose compromise.

Here lay the fatal flaw. Jehu removed what was obviously grotesque while retaining what served state convenience. The land was swept clean of Baal's filth, while the throne remained built upon Jeroboam's calculated idolatry.

God commended his obedience, "Because you have done well in carrying out what is right in my sight, your descendants shall sit upon Israel's throne to the fourth generation" (2 Kings 10:30). But Scripture also includes sober words: "Jehu was never careful to walk in the law of the Lord God of Israel with all his heart" (2 Kings 10:31).

The word "careful" carries weight like a millstone. He possessed passion yet lacked reverence. He wielded zeal while knowing nothing of true devotion. He served God's immediate purposes without ever surrendering to God's deeper heart. While he fulfilled prophecy with ruthless efficiency, he never became the reformer Israel truly needed.

The prophet Hosea would later declare, "In a little while I will punish the house of Jehu for the blood of Jezreel" (Hosea 1:4). This was never a condemnation of the initial divine judgment, but recognition of Jezreel becoming a symbol of violence done in God's name while tainted by human ambition. What should have been holy surgery had become unholy slaughter, divine justice corrupted by political expedience.

Jehu became divine vengeance's vessel while refusing to become divine renewal's agent. His dynasty endured for four generations as promised, while his kingdom crumbled soon after. Jezreel became a byword for judgment itself, a reminder of what begins in divine obedience while ending in human pride.

Every generation finds in his story a sobering truth: it is possible to be anointed by heaven while falling short of heaven's heart, to wield righteous power for unrighteous ends, to execute divine justice while harboring personal ambition. Partial obedience, even if praised for a moment, will ultimately face judgment in full.

The idols serving his own convenience remained standing.

Ultimately, Jehu was a sword in the Almighty's hand—sharp, swift, devastating in its designated task. However, the Hand wielding him mourned over a blade that never learned to rest in close communion with its Master. The fire burning his enemies never warmed his own heart toward the God who had ignited it.

Kingdoms fell before him, while he never conquered himself. The land was cleansed, while his own soul never sought cleansing. A sword knowing no sheath can cut friend and foe alike.

SIMON THE ZEALOT: THE REVOLUTIONARY TRANSFORMED

By the time Jesus walked Galilee's dusty roads, Judea had fallen beneath the eagle's shadow. What had once been the land of patriarchs and kings was now merely another province in Rome's vast empire. They were governed by foreign power, patrolled by foreign legions, and taxed under Caesar's distant authority.

The conquerors had claimed all. Jerusalem's ancient stones bore witness to alien rule, while Jericho and Bethlehem lay under occupation's weight. Herod the Great had worn the title of king as Caesar's creature—a puppet master known for architectural splendor and murderous paranoia. Upon his death, the kingdom was carved among his sons like spoils of war: Archelaus ruling Judea, Herod Antipas governing

Galilee, and Philip holding the northern territories. Above them all stood Roman governors like Pontius Pilate.

Coins bore Caesar's graven image, laws carried Caesar's authority, and Israel's children bore the crushing weight of foreign dominion—taxed into poverty, their movements watched, their words weighed for sedition.

Among the occupied, paths were divided. Many chose collaboration, trading freedom for survival. Others retreated into resignation, waiting for heaven to act while earth grew darker. Still others chose the path of fire and steel.

From among these resisters arose the Zealots—the fierce brotherhood of patriots who believed violent revolution could overthrow Rome and birth God's kingdom on earth. To their burning hearts, bloodshed was a sacred duty rather than a sin. Rome was the new Egypt, its legions the latest taskmasters. The hour of deliverance had surely come.

From their ranks emerged Simon.

The Gospels grant him one defining word, "Simon who was called the Zealot" (Luke 6:15; Acts 1:13). The single title speaks volumes about the man who would follow Christ. Before walking the path of peace, he had known the way of the assassin and underground resistance. Before carrying the cross, he had carried the dagger. Shaped in fury's furnace and sharpened by injustice, he awaited a messiah who would drive the Romans into the sea with sword in hand.

Then Jesus called his name, and everything changed.

The warrior, originally trusting in iron, learned to follow the Lamb of God. Instead of overthrowing Rome, the king he anticipated spoke of loving enemies, forgiving debts, and willingly bearing crosses. The revolution he envisioned was rooted in surrender rather than violence. This Messiah would wash feet instead of spilling blood and hang on a cross rather than seek worldly kingship.

Simon remained when others might have turned away.

Abandoning the blade, he embraced discipleship's weightier burden. Where once he had lived for a violent cause, now he served a Kingdom whose origins lay beyond this world's understanding (John 18:36). His zeal was transformed, redirected from destruction to divine purpose.

Nor did he walk this path alone. Among the twelve stood Matthew, the despised tax collector who had grown wealthy serving Rome's revenue machine. Once, Simon would have marked such a man for death as a traitor. Under Christ's transforming power, they became brothers. Here lay the Gospel's deepest miracle, in the enemies it united beneath one banner as much as the sins it forgave.

Simon did not write a Gospel or a sermon for future generations, nor did he perform recorded miracles that would be remembered through time. Tradition suggests he brought the good news to faraway places—perhaps Persia, Syria, or even Egypt's ancient mysteries or Britain's rugged coast.

His end is described differently: some records say he was crucified like Jesus, while others say he was dismembered to silence his voice. Simon, like many of the apostles, endured with reverence for the eternal kingdom, trading his dagger for armor that mortal weapons could never pierce.

Vengeance shifted to the declaration of peace. His zeal, now fueled by grace, grew stronger and was directed at salvation instead of destruction.

Simon the Zealot serves as an everlasting symbol of redemption's reach, demonstrating that even the most misguided passion can be transformed and empowered through Christ's service. His story encourages every believer that the greatest victories are achieved by breaking down the strongholds that keep human hearts captive.

Once he lived by the blade, dreaming of freedom won through blood. Then he followed the One who was pierced for his sake and the world's salvation.

Simon the Zealot became far greater than any revolutionary who ever drew sword against oppression.

He became an apostle of the Prince of Peace.

JESUS CHRIST: THE WARRIOR OF WARRIORS

The man from Nazareth stands before history with claims magnificent beyond mortal lips, declarations of deity itself. Here walks the One proclaiming Himself resurrection and life, way and truth, the light of the world. Every word resonates with absolute authority. What teacher commanded nature's forces? What philosopher demonstrated power over death? What instructor fulfilled prophecies written centuries before His birth with mathematical precision? Words of teachings of love, mercy, and grace flow from One possessing the divine prerogative to forgive sins and grant eternal life.

Consider the beautiful harmony of claim and character. God incarnate would speak with divine authority while displaying perfect humility. One possessing eternal life would rightfully promise it to others while demonstrating power over death. One deserving worship would receive it with fitting dignity while serving others with divine love. The Jesus emerging from Gospel accounts presents this exact portrait.

Examine the evidence; a magnificent picture emerges. Here stands One whose moral teachings transformed civilizations, whose psychological insights illuminate human nature's deepest chambers, whose understanding of divine truth satisfied the greatest minds across millennia. Here stands One speaking with absolute authority while washing disciples' feet, claiming universal dominion while healing the broken, declaring Himself judge of humanity while dying to redeem those He would judge.

Behold Him as the Warrior walking across eternity's battlefields, His sword shining like captured starlight. He fights against principalities and powers operating in darkness behind the veil, destroying only to save and reclaim His children's hearts. The ancient dragon writhes beneath His heel, death flees at His presence like shadows before dawn, and hell releases its prisoners at His command.

See Him as the Priest, carrying an offering greater than all sacrifices, His crimson blood more valuable than Ophir's gold. His hands, once shaping wood in Nazareth, now bear the stigmata of iron nails, wounds proclaiming mercy to a world overwhelmed by sin. He stands forever between the wrath of sacred justice and the condemnation of fallen humanity, with intercession rising like a gentle breeze. His mediation spans the vast gap between heaven and earth.

Hear Him as the Prophet whose voice echoes with the authority of eternity, with words that bear divine decree and creative power. When He speaks, mountains shake and seas obey, demons scatter into caves, and the dead rise as if awakening from sleep. His prophecies stretch across ages like golden threads woven into history, offering promises that anchor hope and declarations that reshape reality. He speaks of what will be and commands what must be to fulfill divine purpose.

Know Him as the King who reigns by divine right, older than the foundations of the world. His Kingdom advances as hearts are transformed when surrendered souls claim territories in His name. His throne is rooted in righteousness, His scepter rules over all nations, and His dominion will have no end, even when stars grow cold.

Worship before Him as the Judge whose eyes perceive every truth, whose scales weigh every motive with perfect precision, whose verdict determines eternal destiny with absolute finality. His judgment stems from perfect love, with sentences emerging from infinite mercy, and condemnation serving as a gateway to understanding justification. He judges to deliver, separating light from darkness, wheat from chaff, sheep from goats, with omniscience tempered by grace's tenderness.

Rest in Him as the Father whose strong arms can carry His children through any storm and whose gentle heart heals wounds. He gathers orphans to His breast, shelters the vulnerable under His wings, and provides for His children every need from His endless riches of glory. His discipline comes from love, correction from wisdom, and training from a desire to see His children fulfilled in their purpose.

Here stands the Christ descending from heaven's throne to earth's manger, compressing infinite into finite, clothing omnipotence in flesh tender as a child's.

In Nazareth's rolling hills, He worked with hands growing calloused and strong, shaping wood with fingers that had traced planetary orbits and set the sea's boundaries. He understood the honest ache of toil, the satisfaction of a job well done, and the fellowship of men earning bread by sweat. Even in those hidden years, divine glory shone through human ordinariness—wisdom astonishing teachers, understanding leaving the learned speechless, character perfect—even enemies could find no fault in Him.

When the time arrived, He stepped out from the hidden years into three years of powerful ministry. Divine power moved through dusty villages and busy streets. Demons fled at His command. Storms calmed at His voice. The dead rose when He called. The carpenter's son revealed Himself as the Creator of all things. He spoke with authority that made religious leaders tremble and drew crowds by the thousands. He touched lepers and healed them. He spoke to paralyzed men, and they walked. He fed large crowds with a few scraps and gathered leftovers in baskets.

Yet with every miracle, every teaching, every clash with religious pride, the shadow of the cross grew closer. The same hands that could have summoned armies of angels would soon be nailed to wood. The voice that commanded nature would cry out in agony for a world that had lost its way. All that power, enough to shake heaven and earth, would be poured out as sacrifice.

"It is finished" (John 19:30). This cry resonates across the universe, heralding triumph. The debt was paid, the curse was lifted, the path was made clear, and victory was achieved. Death had consumed the Life-giver, only to find that Life had already conquered death from within.

Three days later, the tomb surrendered its Prisoner. Resurrection was revelation— the unveiling of power that had always been there, demonstrating authority that death could never challenge, proving this Man was indeed God in flesh.

Now He reigns from heaven's throne, having ascended to rule. His current reign is lively—interceding for His people, expanding His Kingdom, and getting ready for His return. The hands that were nailed to the cross now hold the keys of the universe, the voice that cried in anguish now commands legions of angels, and the One who died in weakness now lives with the power of resurrection.

His return approaches soon. Yet until the appointed day arrives, His Kingdom advances through ordinary men transformed by extraordinary grace.

In Him, every promise receives its "Yes," every hope is fulfilled, and every longing is satisfied. He is the desire of nations, the hope of glory, the author and finisher of faith. Before Him, all knees shall bow; at His name, all tongues shall confess; and in His presence, every tear will be wiped away.

In His name, demons tremble and flee, angels worship and adore, the redeemed sing with voices like many waters. The Carpenter of Nazareth stands revealed as Creator of all things. The suffering Servant shows forth as sovereign Lord. The slain Lamb reigns as living Lion.

He was before all things, and from Him all things exist. He is the image of the invisible God, the firstborn over all creation. Of His Kingdom, there shall be no end (Luke 1:33).

This eternal truth echoes through time's corridors and resounds in heaven's halls. What mortal king can make such claims? What earthly empire has escaped its crumbling to dust? Yet here stands the King whose Kingdom was established before the world's foundation and shall endure when the last star burns cold.

On that magnificent and glorious day when He appears in majesty, every eye shall see Him—those who pierced Him, those who worship Him, those who rejected Him, and those who embraced Him. The skies will be rolled back, the earth will tremble, and mountains will melt like wax in His presence. He will judge the world righteously, distinguishing wheat from chaff, sheep from goats, with perfect judgment driven by omniscient love.

Even now, as we await His glorious appearance, our hearts cry out: "Even so, come quickly, Lord Jesus!" This is the heartfelt plea of every believer and the eager expectation of every soul that has experienced His goodness. The Spirit and bride say, "Come!" Let every receptive heart repeat the same prayer: "Come!" Come and establish Your Kingdom in its fullness. Come and make all things new. Come and receive the reward for Your sufferings. Come quickly, for our souls yearn for the fulfillment of all You have promised.

The voice that once cried from the cross, "It is finished!" now proclaims from glory's throne, "Surely I come quickly." He who cannot lie has spoken this; He who knows the end from the beginning has declared it; He who controls times and seasons has decreed it. The return is guaranteed, timing is perfect, and glory is assured.

Therefore, let every tongue confess and every heart believe: Jesus Christ is Lord, to the glory of God the Father. He is Alpha and Omega, the Beginning and the End, the First and the Last. He is the Way, the Truth, and the Life. He is King of Kings, Lord of Lords, and Warrior of Warriors, and His name shall endure forever. His throne will last from generation to generation, and His Kingdom will be forever lasting. Come, Lord Jesus. Come quickly!

The call has thundered through the ages. From heaven's heights to earth's shadows, from patriarch to prophet, from judge to king, the summons remains unchanged: rise, endure, war for what is holy.

These men answered when their hour came. Each in his appointed time. Each in his chosen way. Each marked forever by the fire of the One who called his name.

The same voice echoes today. The same King who summoned Abraham from Ur, who blazed from the burning bush before Moses, who anointed David in forgotten fields, who transformed Simon the Zealot into an apostle—He still calls.

The brotherhood spans centuries. The mission burns bright. The ancient war rages on.

In this very moment, He is calling your name.

Will you answer?

BENEDICTION

Come Holy Spirit. Come Holy Spirit. Come Holy Spirit. Come Lord Jesus Christ. Come Lord Jesus Christ. Come Lord Jesus Christ. Come Father Yahweh. Come Father Yahweh. Come Father Yahweh.

Hosanna in the highest! Blessed is He who comes in the name of the Lord. The King of kings has arrived. The Lord of lords has defeated death. The Warrior of warriors has vanquished the dragon.

Lord Jesus Christ, Son of the most-high Yahweh, redeem the warrior reading these words. Fill and anoint the warrior with the Blood of Christ. Fill and anoint the warrior with the Living Water of Yahweh. Align the warrior's footsteps with the path of Christ. Cover Your warrior with immaculate armor of God, so that no evil may prevail against the warrior and the domain he cares for.

Blessed Holy Trinity, though many feel lost, with You all of humanity is recovered. With Your blessing and abundance, compliment the domains of all Your children. Oh, Divine Creator, inspire this reader to go forth and produce fruit aligned with the Your heavenly will.

May this warrior, and all Your warriors of Christ, be blessed with the abundance and prosperity to go forth and make disciples of all nations. May the warrior never lack resource, may they never lack Your divine mercy, forgiveness, or guidance.

Father Yahweh, you have known each warrior since the beginning of time. You created their names in the Book of Life. Allow Your children to fulfill Your mission. Allow Your creation to sing Your praises with the blessings You bestowed upon them.

May the warriors of Christ go forth always being in the correct location and the correct time for the ministry of the Father to be revealed. May the steps, words, and actions of the warrior of Christ be anointed by the Father.

In the name and power of the Holy Trinity, the three-in-one triune Lord, may all who read this text go forth in the divine domain and protection from the Highest. May the warrior walk invincibly in the light of Christ forever and ever.

In the name of the Father, the Son, and the Holy Spirit may the kingdom of heaven divinely protect, educate, and guide all warriors of Christ to go forth in the name of the King, as the King's Warriors. Amen.

BIBLIOGRAPHY

PRIMARY SOURCE

The Holy Bible. English Standard Version. Crossway Bibles, 2016.

SECONDARY SOURCES

Books

Bonhoeffer, Dietrich. *The Cost of Discipleship*. Touchstone, 1995.

Lewis, C. S. *Mere Christianity*. HarperOne, 2001.

Lewis, C. S. *The Problem of Pain*. HarperOne, 2001.

Lewis, C. S. *The Weight of Glory and Other Addresses*. HarperOne, 2001.

MacArthur, John. *The MacArthur Study Bible*. Thomas Nelson, 2006.

Nouwen, Henri J. M. *In the Name of Jesus: Reflections on Christian Leadership*. Crossroad Publishing, 1989.

Strong, James. *The New Strong's Exhaustive Concordance of the Bible*. Thomas Nelson, 1996.

Tolkien, J. R. R. *The Lord of the Rings*. Houghton Mifflin, 2004.

Tolkien, J. R. R. *The Silmarillion*. Houghton Mifflin, 1977.

Tozer, A. W. *The Knowledge of the Holy: The Attributes of God: Their Meaning in the Christian Life*. Moody Publishers, 1961.

Tozer, A. W. *The Pursuit of God*. Moody Publishers, 1948.

Tozer, A. W. *The Root of the Righteous*. Moody Publishers, 1955.

Articles and Digital Media

Welch, Taylor. "You Do Not Have to Be Famous to Build a Kingdom Legacy." *The Deep End*, Substack newsletter, July 11, 2023. https://taylorawelch.substack.com/p/you-dont-have-to-be-famous-to-build.

Welch, Taylor. *The Deep End*. YouTube video, 1:22:42. July 18, 2023. https://www.youtube.com/watch?v=28Is22w68vc.

Liturgical and Reference Works

The Book of Common Prayer. Church Publishing Incorporated, various editions.

SCRIPTURE REFERENCES

GENESIS: 3:8, 3:15, 12:1, 14:19, 14:22–23, 15:5, 15:6, 15:16, 16:7–13, 17:5, 17:15–16, 18:19, 19:37, 19:38, 22:2, 22:12, 22:16–18

EXODUS: 1:8, 1:8–14, 1:22, 2:3, 2:10, 2:11–12, 2:14, 2:15, 3:6–10, 3:11, 3:14, 4:10, 4:12, 4:14–16, 5:1, 7:10, 7:12, 7:20–21, 8:6, 8:17, 8:24, 9:6, 9:10, 9:25, 10:15, 10:22–23, 12:29–30, 13:21, 13:21–22, 15:3, 16:4, 17:6, 17:8–13, 24:13, 33:11

LEVITICUS: 26:8

NUMBERS: 13:1–2, 13:8, 13:27–33, 13:30, 13:31, 14:8–9, 14:24, 14:30, 14:33–34, 21:21–26, 25:7–8, 27:18, 32:12

DEUTERONOMY: 2:10–11, 2:19, 8:2, 12:31, 34:5–6

JOSHUA: 1:7–8, 5:13–15, 6:1–20, 6:20, 10:13, 12:24, 14:6, 14:10–12, 14:12, 14:15, 18–19, 21:45, 24:15, 24:29–30, 24:31

JUDGES: 3:15, 3:19, 3:20, 3:21–23, 3:29, 3:30, 6:1–6, 6:12, 6:15, 6:16, 6:21, 6:37, 6:39, 6:40, 7:2–7, 7:16–22, 11:2, 11:3, 11:14–27, 11:29, 11:30–31, 11:34, 11:37, 11:39, 11:40, 13:25, 14:6, 15:14–15, 16:6, 16:16, 16:17, 16:22, 16:28, 16:30, 21:25

1 SAMUEL: 1:11, 8:5, 9:2, 10:1, 13:8–14, 13:14, 14:47–48, 15:9–23, 15:11, 16:12, 17:7, 17:34–35, 17:45, 24:6, 24:10, 31:3–6

2 SAMUEL: 1:25, 8:18, 12:13

1 KINGS: 1:38–39, 2:25, 2:28–34, 2:35, 2:44–46, 12:28–30, 21:23

2 KINGS: 9:6–7, 9:20, 9:30–37, 10:27, 10:30, 10:31

1 CHRONICLES: 11:22, 11:23

2 CHRONICLES: 16:9

JOB: 1:6–7

PSALMS: 1:1–3, 16:11, 23:1, 24:8, 32:3, 51, 51:10, 78:70–72, 110:4, 119:9, 119:11, 119:133, 144:1

PROVERBS: 4:23, 21:31, 24:10, 27:17

ECCLESIASTES: 4:12

ISAIAH: 11:1, 14:13–14, 42:13, 50:7, 53:6, 55:11

JEREMIAH: 7:31, 17:9, 29:11

EZEKIEL: 28:14

DANIEL: 3:25, 12:1

HOSEA: 1:4

MICAH: 6:8

MATTHEW: 4:1–11, 5:8, 5:16, 6:33, 7:24, 7:29, 10:34, 11:29, 15:19–20, 25:21, 27:45–51

MARK: 8:34

LUKE: 1:33, 2:1–7, 6:15, 7:22, 9:23, 10:18, 15:4, 22:42–44

JOHN: 1:1, 1:14, 1:29, 2:15–17, 3:17, 13:3–5, 14:6, 14:27, 15:4, 18:36, 19:30, 21:15–17

ACTS: 1:9–11, 1:13, 4:13, 7:22

ROMANS: 1:17, 5:3–4, 8:1, 8:28, 8:34, 12:1–2, 13:14

1 CORINTHIANS: 4:2, 6:18, 6:19, 9:24, 10:4, 11:1, 15:58, 16:13

2 CORINTHIANS: 5:17, 10:3–5, 10:5, 12:9

GALATIANS: 2:20, 5:22–23

EPHESIANS: 2:8–9, 2:10, 4:32, 6:10–18, 6:11, 6:16

PHILIPPIANS: 1:6, 2:9, 2:12–13, 3:13–14, 4:8, 4:13

COLOSSIANS: 1:16–17, 3:23

1 THESSALONIANS: 5:8, 5:17

2 THESSALONIANS: 3:10

1 TIMOTHY: 2:21, 4:7–8, 6:12

2 TIMOTHY: 1:7, 2:3–4, 2:15, 4:7

TITUS: 2:11–14

HEBREWS: 1:3, 4:12, 5:8, 7:1–3, 9:12, 10:24–25, 11:19, 11:32, 12:1–2, 12:28, 13:8, 13:17

JAMES: 1:12, 1:22, 4:7

1 PETER: 1:6–7, 2:9, 5:8

2 PETER: 1:3

1 JOHN: 3:8, 4:4

JUDE: 1:3

REVELATION: 1:8, 4:10, 5:5, 5:6, 5:12, 12:4, 12:7–8, 12:9, 19:11–16, 20:10, 21:5

AUTHOR BIOGRAPHY

MATTHEW PATRICK HUGHES, CSCS, is a Christian martial artist, strength and conditioning coach, and former collegiate football player who has dedicated his life to developing servant warriors of Christ—physically, mentally, and spiritually.

He holds a Bachelor of Science in Sport Administration from Louisiana State University and is a Certified Strength and Conditioning Specialist through the National Strength and Conditioning Association. His journey has taken him through the world of college athletics, national championship-level coaching internships, and years of mentoring others in the weight room, on the mat, and beyond.

But Matthew's true qualifications come not from titles or achievements, but from transformation. His life has been shaped by testing, refined by grace, and redirected by the faithful hand of God. Through every season, Christ has remained his anchor and guide.

His love for martial arts—Brazilian Jiu-Jitsu, Muay Thai, and boxing—is more than a craft. It is a place where truth is revealed, discipline is forged, and the deeper spiritual battle comes into focus. For Matthew, strength is most powerful when it is surrendered. True manhood begins with humility. And the greatest victories are not won in crowds, but in the quiet moments of prayer and obedience before the King.

The King's Warrior is more than a book—it is a calling. And Matthew is not only its author. He is its first witness.